Bringing the Kingdom

Bringing the Kingdom

Progressive Reflections on Scripture

KEVIN BROWN

RESOURCE *Publications* · Eugene, Oregon

BRINGING THE KINGDOM
Progressive Reflections on Scripture

Resource Publications
An Imprint of Wipf and Stock Publishers
199 W. 8th Ave., Suite 3
Eugene, OR 97401

www.wipfandstock.com

PAPERBACK ISBN: 978-1-5326-1955-7
HARDCOVER ISBN: 978-1-4982-4591-3
EBOOK ISBN: 978-1-4982-4590-6

Manufactured in the U.S.A.   DECEMBER 21, 2017

For everyone who has shown me how to work for the kingdom
and where I so often fail to do so

Contents

Introduction

T HIS BOOK CAME OUT of a Sunday school class I was in a couple of years
ago. We were reading selections of a book structured much like this
one: short sections reflecting on one or two passages. Rather than using the
lectionary calendar, as I do, this author went through the Bible in the order
it's published. I liked the general structure and set up of the book, but there
was something nagging at me every week we used one of the sections to
guide our discussions.

I attend a rather progressive church in the Presbyterian Church
(U.S.A.) denomination. We have a female minister, and we have several
LGBTQ members, including at least a couple who are elders. The leader
of our Sunday school for that particular study was a retired former minister who's a gay male. We purposefully work to be open, affirming, and
inclusive. However, the book we were reading seemed to go only so far; the
author would hint at ideas related to Jesus's radical inclusivity, but then not
pursue them. I left most days frustrated at how close we came to talking
about these ideas without quite getting there.

I grew up in a Presbyterian Church (U.S.A.) congregation, but it was
moderate to conservative. We had a minister who was formerly Baptist, and
the church was in a conservative town, which skewed even most progressive denominations that direction. As a teenager, I went to an Independent
Christian Church (the moderate branch of the Church of Christ/Christian
churches; we had music, but no women in leadership) because of their
youth group, but that led me (by my own decision; no one forced me into
it) into an eight-year (or so) stretch of fundamentalism. I took the Bible
literally, listened only to Christian music, and, for a time, watched only
Christian movies and no television.

I even went to a college associated with the Independent Christian Church, as I planned to become a youth minister. Those years did provide me with a solid biblical education, even if I ultimately moved away from the interpretations I heard throughout that time. I ultimately left the denomination and church, as I began asking questions that not only had no satisfactory answers, but which led people (one youth minister, in particular) to tell me to stop asking questions. I was out of the church for four (or so) years. While I wouldn't recommend people leave the church, it helped me considerably, as I was able to come back to my faith with a new perspective.

I came back in through writers my younger self would have believed to be heretics, people who took a more scholarly approach to the Bible, Jesus, and faith, in general. I had done some reading in other religions—Buddhism, especially—which also helped shape my thinking. Most importantly, I found University Presbyterian Church, a church in Tuscaloosa, Alabama, where I could ask questions, and people would take them seriously, encouraging me to explore them. The year after that, I moved to Macon, Georgia, where I attended First Christian Church (Disciples of Christ), another church that gave me freedom to explore my questions and resources to support that search. For the past eight years, I've attended Northminster Presbyterian Church in Chattanooga, TN.[1] As with the previous two churches, I've found people here who encourage me and others to delve into uncomfortable ideas, supporting us as we do so. I couldn't have become the Christian and thinker I am today without these churches and a number of people there.

While I'm not a trained minister and have not attended seminary, I have spent much of my adult life reading and studying, often teaching Sunday school classes. Thus, I've written this book for lay people, particularly for Sunday school classes, who want to explore what it means to be a progressive Christian in the twenty-first century. I've structured the book using the liturgical calendar, so the book lends itself to short sessions during seasons like Advent, Lent, or Easter. Classes could use it for longer periods of time, as well, or individuals could use it as a weekly reading to provoke thought in their lives.

Overall, my hope is simply that this book will help anyone who wants to explore the more progressive side of Christianity. I needed a book like this one when I was coming back into the church, so I hope you find it as

1. A special thanks to our minister, Rev. Laura Becker, for reading this manuscript and providing helpful and challenging feedback.

useful as I believe I would have. If nothing else, I hope that it reminds us all that God can handle any questions we might have, that it's not just acceptable to ask those questions, God encourages us to do so. The church should be a place of welcome, a place where we can find grace and mercy and love, no matter who we are, what we have experienced, and where we are in life. I've tried to write this book to remind us of those truths.

It's the End of the World As We Know It

First Sunday in Advent

Matthew 24:36–44
Romans 13:8–14

F OR MOST OF US on the more progressive end of the religious spectrum, any talk of apocalypse becomes problematic quite quickly. First, for those of us who grew up or spent time in more fundamentalist, evangelical circles, we have all too vivid memories of sermons talking about the end times and how, somehow always, we were living in them. We had signs and wonders pointed out to us, showing how they matched up with Daniel or Revelation, making it clear that the end of the world was just around the corner. We watched awful movies in the 1980s that portrayed what would happen when Jesus returned (usually involving children coming into houses to find no one there, an image that might have leeched into our own lives), and, of course, there was the *Left Behind* book series. I've even heard some people describe "rapture practice," where they would do deep knee-bends, then rise up, lifting their hands to the heavens, as they imagined they might be carried away one day. We might have even bought and read Hal Lindsey's book showing exactly how everything matched up with passages from the apocalyptic sections of the Bible, so we were quite clear on how the end of the world would occur. Not surprisingly, those predictions never came true, which often led us to question our faith, given that our faith was built on the Bible's being an accurate forecaster of future events, as if it is our Christian Nostradamus.

There's a larger problem, though, in that, for many of us, we don't think about the afterlife in the same way as evangelicals. We might not believe in any kind of literal second coming (or even a metaphorical one), and we might even go so far as to question the existence of any kind of heaven. Instead, we argue that heaven happens here on Earth when we act out the teachings of Jesus, and that hell is simply an invention of the medieval church designed to control the masses. I might be going a bit far, of course, but it's not a stretch to say that most progressive Christians struggle when it comes to talking about anything related to Jesus's (or the rest of the Bible's) apocalyptic passages, as they usually ascribe them simply to the culture the Bible comes from when people quite clearly believed in a coming apocalypse of some sort.

Thus, we're left with what to do with these passages. I'm never comfortable simply dismissing passages as presenting archaic beliefs that have nothing to teach us, as there are almost always truths lying beneath the surface of those passages, and I definitely believe that to be the case here. One of the reasons our society is so focused on apocalyptic scenes (note the number of zombie shows and movies that have replaced the focus on nuclear annihilation prevalent in the 1980s) is that we all will ultimately suffer from our personal apocalypse: we will all die. The world will come to an end for us, so, whether we want to admit this truth about ourselves, we believe the world will, for all purposes, end. We are unable to truly imagine a world without us in it, as our viewpoint is the only one we know and can imagine.

Thus, if we want a different way of thinking about the afterlife, we can think about the world that will exist after us. Samuel Scheffler, author of *Death & the Afterlife*, takes an interesting approach to this subject. He doesn't believe in the afterlife in the traditional sense, but he does talk about a literal world that exists after our deaths, as the earth will continue after we die. He then proceeds to argue that, if we were to ignore that world, it would change almost everything about our lives. He uses the example of a cancer researcher to ask whether that would be a good use of time and resources if everyone on the planet was simply going to die out in seventy or eighty years; why would anyone do research that will not see real results in their lifetime? He even references a scene from *Annie Hall*, where Alvy Singer, a nine-year-old, says that he won't do his homework because the universe will end. The doctor assures him that that end will not happen for billions of years, but Scheffler asks whether or not Alvy would be right if all lives would end in ten or twenty years. Essentially, he's taking the idea of what we would do if we only had six months (or two decades) to live, but complicating it by removing any future generations.

It is these future generations that might help us better understand what Jesus and Paul are getting at here, as opposed to the more traditional view of the afterlife. Rather than wanting us to live a certain way to get into heaven, Jesus wants us to live a certain way to affect those around us and those who will come after us, those who will live on in what we can call our personal afterlife. Even if we don't have children, we have an impact on the world that exists after we cease to, whether that impact is large or small. We should "keep awake," as Jesus says, because we never know when our world will end and our impact will cease.

This unexpectedness, combined with that impact, leads to Paul's passage on loving one another. He, too, wants us to wake up, to move from darkness into light, but he is more explicit about what he means by that. He wants us to love our neighbor, as that is "the fulfilling of the law." Loving those around us will have ripple effects, changing the world that we leave behind, not in any sense of cheesy funeral scenes from movies, but by truly changing people around us, causing them to live different lives, as well. If we believe that we will one day die and cease to exist and that we don't know when that will occur, we should live in the light Paul talks about, loving our neighbors. We might or might not exist in some sort of heaven above, but we can help those who come after us to live in a world that is closer to heaven, giving our lives more meaning than we can now imagine.

Questions for Reflection or Discussion:

How do you think about apocalyptic passages in the Bible today?

What are ways we can live out loving others that will live on after us?

The Harbinger of Things to Come

Second Sunday in Advent

Luke 3:1–14

I'VE OFTEN WONDERED IF John the Baptizer could find a job as a minister. His wardrobe and eating habits certainly wouldn't endear him to any kind of pastoral search committee (I can just imagine their taking him out to dinner when he arrived for the interview), but I also think his message would take him out of contention. Most ministers who begin their sermons with "You brood of vipers! Who warned you to flee from the wrath to come?" don't last all that long.

Many scholars believe that John was a member of the Essene community, a Jewish sect that lived outside of cities who devoted themselves to purity and an ascetic lifestyle. In fact, some scholars go even farther and argue that John is the one who changed the Essene lifestyle into something different, which ultimately became Christianity. They point to the fact that there was the same communal lifestyle we later see in the book of Acts, as Essenes lived in communities where they held everything in common. Their belief in purity led to a firm belief in baptism or bathing, which continued on into Christianity in a way it hadn't in Judaism. The Essenes eschewed marriage out of an avoidance of uncleanness, and the early Christians also avoided marriage, though they did so because they believed the second coming of Jesus could occur at any time.

There are other similarities: a belief in the power of prophecy; a similar system of organization; similar rules for people who traveled to do charity work (as when Jesus sends his disciples out with only the clothes they are wearing). Most importantly, though, the Essenes took part in love-feasts, which the early Christians continued and connected to what we now call the Last Supper. A few scholars go beyond connecting John to the Essene community and put forth the idea that Jesus had been an Essene, which is why John was familiar with him. Others take issue with that connection, given that Jesus seems anti-ascetic in many places, and he was clearly not concerned with rules of purity and cleanliness, given his willingness to break Jewish rules on those subjects.

Regardless of whether or not all of these connections lead us to connect John or Jesus to the Essene community, it's clear that John's teaching is quite similar to theirs. The first part of John's teaching is the most familiar, in fact, when he warns his listeners that their connection to Abraham, and, thus, their Judaism, will not save them. In preparing the way for Jesus, John is bringing the ax to the root of the tree, as he puts it, showing that God's love will be for all people, not simply for the Jews. By taking up the metaphor of the ax, though, his message seems to emphasize judgment over love.

The similar passages in Matthew and Luke stop with this teaching, leaving us with an image of John as a wild-eyed prophet who seems bent on bringing some cleansing of Judaism, wanting nothing more than to wipe it clean, so Jesus can start from scratch. However, John's message is much more than that, as he is setting up the main ideas that Jesus will explore in his ministry. Whether that connection comes from their similar backgrounds in the Essene community or because they had spoken at some point before (they are cousins, according to several gospel accounts) or simply because God had given them the same message to bring to the people, John's influence is clear.

First, the Isaiah passage sets up the idea that God's love is for all people, and the path to that love is being made clear and easy. In a culture where everyone walked or rode donkeys everywhere they went, the idea that valleys would be filled and mountains would be made low would be appealing. God is making their journey as easy as possible, as it will be straight and smooth and flat. Because of the message that John (and then Jesus) is bringing, it will be possible for all of humanity to see the salvation of God. This quote from Isaiah is much more about the love of God than the judgment of God.

Second, the part that the author of Luke adds that is not found in the other two gospels lays out how we can see the kingdom of God here on earth, as well as in heaven. After John makes the proclamation about the ax's being at the root of the trees, his listeners, rightly moved by such a statement, ask what they can do. John doesn't respond by talking about following the Jewish laws or by offering the correct sacrifices at the temple. Like the Old Testament prophets, he wants to take the people beyond that point, to show them what God truly requires.

Here is what scholars see as a major connection to the Essenes, in that John is essentially promoting communal living without suggesting people leave their families and live together. He is laying out the same idea that Jesus will put forth in the parable of the sheep and the goats, among other places. John wants his listeners (and us) to set aside the belief that what we own is our own and see that the way to the kingdom is to remember that all we have belongs to each other and to God.

When people from the crowd ask him what they should do, he simply responds that they should give out of their plenty to those who lack the basic necessities of life. If people don't have clothing or shelter or food, and we do, we should give it to them. When different sub-groups ask for clarification, he tells them not to cheat people or extort money from them, reminding them to be satisfied with what they already have. Note he's not saying we should not seek a living wage, as the soldiers who ask the question were already paid enough to live; instead, he's saying that they should not take money from those who are already struggling under the oppression of Rome for their own benefit.

John lays out an outline for the kingdom of God that Jesus will take up again and again. The only way the hungry get fed is for us to feed them. When we are focused only on our desires, then the way to God is not straight and easy, as we are the ones making it more difficult. We take the path God has made smooth, and we make it crooked and rough. Whether we call God's straight path communism or Essene or charity or simply love, it is the main message John gives to those who ask how to live, and it's the reoccurring theme that Jesus will return to again and again throughout his ministry.

Questions for Reflection or Discussion:

What in our lives prevents us from living out John's radical message?

What might John say to various contemporary professions if they asked him what they should do?

Do You Hear?

Third Sunday in Advent

Matthew 11:2–15
Isaiah 35:1–10

A s a teacher, I'm always fascinated by how Jesus answers questions (or, in reality, how he doesn't answer them). In the passage from Matthew, John the Baptizer has sent messengers to Jesus to see if he is, in fact, the Messiah, or if there is someone else John should be waiting for. Even before we get to the question, though, the writer of Matthew tips us off a bit by saying, "When John heard in prison what the Messiah was doing . . . " There doesn't seem to be any kind of suspense here as to whether or not Jesus is the Messiah; the fact that this passage comes just under halfway through Matthew certainly helps with that.

However, that mention of the word *Messiah* before the question lets us know something else that will come up in Jesus's answer to the question: John already knows what Jesus has been doing. The opening phrase tells us that John's followers have communicated to him what Jesus has been doing, and the author of the gospel describes that as what the Messiah has been doing. John is well aware of what Jesus has been up to, and he doesn't ask that question. Instead, he wants to know, point blank, if Jesus is the Messiah or not, even though he already really knows that Jesus is the Messiah. It seems that John is just having trouble admitting it to himself at this point.

That brings us to Jesus's answer to the question. As he often does, Jesus doesn't answer the question that's asked, as he never says whether he is or isn't the Messiah. Instead, he tells John's followers to go back to John and tell him what he's been doing: healing the blind, the lame, the lepers, and the deaf; raising the dead; proclaiming good news to the poor. Remember, though, that John knows Jesus has been doing all of these actions; that's why John sent his messengers to Jesus in the first place. Essentially, Jesus's answer to John is nothing more than a confirmation of what John already knows, and Jesus seems to think this answer is perfectly acceptable. As far as we can tell in this and other gospel passages, John's followers don't seem bothered by it, either.

The most important part of Jesus's answer, though, might come at the beginning of his response, not the section on what Jesus has done. He first responds, "Go and tell John what you hear and see . . . " Jesus uses these images of hearing and seeing on a regular basis, often with the phrase at the end of this passage: "Let anyone with ears listen!" Perhaps, rather than telling John and his followers all that he has been doing, Jesus is reminding John that he needs to hear and see through God's eyes, as it is only then that he can truly hear and see the work of God in the world. John's question shows that he needs confirmation (as we all do, so often), so it is not Jesus's actions that will convince John; it is Jesus's reminder of how to see the world that will do so.

That same approach happens in Isaiah, as the positive actions happen early in the passage when the wilderness, dry land, and desert all break forth into bloom, revealing the glory of the Lord. It isn't until later in the passage, though, that people shall see and hear; the glory of the Lord has already been around, but the people haven't seen it yet. Once they do see it, then more goodness follows that recognition, as now those dry places are filled with life-giving water, leading to everlasting joy. What the people needed, though, was the ability to hear and see what they should have already known.

Too often, we behave the same way. There is goodness in the world, redemptive acts happening all around us—from organizations that work to end hunger or discrimination to individuals who forgive those who have harmed them or who work for peace between warring nations—yet we are unable to see or hear them. We have moved from seeing the world through God's eyes to seeing the world through a purely materialistic lens. We see acts of social equality—the Supreme Court's decision to legalize same sex marriage, for example—as nothing more than humanity's way of trying to level out a playing field that has been uneven for centuries. We see social justice work—from soup kitchens to protests for a living wage—as nothing more than trying to feed people's bodies or help people find jobs. Like John and his followers, all we see is that Jesus heals people in a variety of ways.

All of those actions are good and necessary and valuable, but we need to see what is behind them to see and hear why they matter; otherwise, we're nothing more than social workers rather than people working for the kingdom here on Earth. Too often, that lack of insight leads to frustration and despair and burnout, rather than leading to the everlasting joy described in Isaiah. It's not simply that we are working to feed people or to create a more equal and just world, it's that we are doing so because of God's redemptive love for humanity, because God loves all equally and wants us to act on that love for all of God's creation. We need to see and hear God in all we do to provide meaning to those actions we do every day to make the world what God can already see and hear.

Questions for Reflection or Discussion:

What do we already know that we often forget?

What are some actions in your life, church, and the world that you often overlook or fail to see as God's work?

A Song for Progressives
Fourth Sunday in Advent

Luke 1:39–56
Micah 5:2–5a

MARY'S MAGNIFICAT (SO NAMED for the first word of her poetic passage in Latin) is one of the standards of progressive Christianity. One of my former ministers used to talk about how every Christian (and many churches) has a "gospel within the gospel," that passage or passages that we return to again and again. In some ways, those passages define who we are in a way that other parts don't. Admitting we have favorite parts of the Bible is a bit like parents' admitting they have a favorite child, but most of us do. Mary's Magnificat is that passage for many progressive Christians, and for good reason.

This part of the Bible is one of the clearest declarations of God's devotion to the poor, the outcast, the hungry, the marginal. Add to that the fact that it comes from Mary immediately after Elizabeth has proclaimed her to be the mother of the Lord, and it becomes quite powerful. Given that this passage so clearly echoes many of the Old Testament prophets, the author of Luke puts Mary in the line of those prophets, raising who we believe to be a poor woman to the position of people like Isaiah and Jeremiah, those who speak on behalf of God. The author also puts this proclamation in the first chapter of the book, clearly laying out this gospel's concern with all of those on the margins of society in first century Israel.

Mary's prophecy, though, is different from those who have come before her. It's true that she shows the same concern for those who need God's protection, talking about the lowly and the hungry, but her verb tense separates her from the Old Testament prophets we tend to think of. While they (like in the passage from Micah) talk about what *shall* happen, Mary talks about what has already happened in the past, what God *has done* already. Such an approach puts her more in line with Miriam whose song (albeit much shorter) in Exodus 15 talks about what God did for the people of Israel in bringing them across the Red Sea and out of Egypt safely. Miriam is the first woman in the Bible to have the title of prophet applied to her, beginning the lineage that Mary is clearly working within.

There are two different ways Mary's use of past tense make sense, both of which should give hope and encouragement to those who work for justice in the world. The first is that God's action of choosing Mary to be the mother of Jesus has already set the world straight, despite the fact that there is still so much injustice. God's choosing Mary sends a message to those in power that their power is fleeting, ephemeral, and not true power at all. When Mary says that God has "brought down the powerful from their thrones," she means that they have lost whatever power they thought they had, but they don't know it yet (and might never know it, as they do not see or hear properly).

We see this past tense nature in contemporary society, especially in America. We have politicians who make laws that try to keep people apart, deprive people of their rights, or actively harm the least powerful among us. They believe they have the real power in this society. However, those who work for justice know that such power, even such laws, will not last, that the ideals of true freedom and equality will win out in the future; it's just a matter of time and effort. President Trump's travel ban on those from majority Muslim countries caused serious disruptions for hundreds and thousands of people, but people, the ones with the real power, stood up and continue to stand up against such division. Those people believe they will win, in the long term.

The other way, a better reading, is to see Mary's proclamation in line with Miriam's, a celebration of all that God has done, which implies what God will do in the future. God's choosing Mary to be Jesus's mother reminds readers of other times God has lifted up the lowly, such as when David becomes Israel's king, or when God satisfied the hungry, such as when he gave the Israelites manna and quail and water. Mary is a Jewish woman, so she knows the history of her people, and she knows the history of her God's protection. She also knows Micah's prophecy that the one who will come forth to rule "shall be great," which means that "he shall be the one of peace." She knows that God seeks relationship with all of humanity, and she knows that God seeks right relationships within humanity. The only person who could lead on behalf of God is "the one of peace."

Those who work for justice, especially when discouraged, must look to the past and see all that has happened over the decades and centuries to see that progress does come, though there is much work to be done. We must remember the women in the late 1800s who met at Seneca Falls, who ultimately led to women's right to vote. We must remember the men and women who sat at lunch counters, who marched through streets, who were beaten and even killed to begin to change the way people treat minorities in this country. We must remember the LGBTQ women and men who rioted outside of the Stonewall Inn who began to say that they would not allow police or anyone else to treat them as inferior any longer. God has given people strength to stand up to those who oppress, to lift up the lowly, to take steps toward progress.

As with Mary's Magnificat, though, looking to the past does not imply that work is done. Her proclamation comes at the beginning of the gospel, before Jesus has spoken a word. It is a celebration of what God has done to show what God will continue to do through women like Mary and Elizabeth and men like Jesus and John. The kingdom comes through people the world overlooks, the poor women who give birth with little fanfare, the people who stand up to say that what is happening is wrong and must stop. God "has brought down the powerful from their thrones," and God will continue to do so through people who hear Mary's voice and carry on her work. The work for such justice will always continue as new groups carry on work began decades, if not centuries, before, but Mary's song reminds us that God's justice eventually carries the day.

Questions for Reflection or Discussion:

Where do we see other examples of people who worked for justice in the past?

What are the main areas we still need to focus on, whether locally, nationally, or internationally?

More Than a Good Story

Christmas Eve

Matthew 1:18–25
I John 4:7–16

THE VIRGIN BIRTH IS one of those milestones in Christianity that pro-
vokes a wide array of feelings in believers and non-believers, alike.
There's a wide range of interpretations: the fundamentalist, evangelical
view that this miracle is one of the key signs that Jesus is the Son of God,
the Messiah who will save Israel; the moderate view that, while something
about this birth was special in that God has come to Earth in human form
out of love for humanity, some scholars translate *virgin* as *young girl*, as it
usually is in Isaiah, so this birth is not miraculous, but still a major event;
then there are those on the extreme ends of Christianity (or even outside of
the faith) who say this story is completely mythical, nothing more than an
attempt to align Jesus with the traditional deities of the day, who always had
some sort of miraculous birth themselves, often with a god involved, maybe
even going so far as to argue that the story is a cover for a more salacious
story of a woman who gives birth to a child out of wedlock.

Those of us in mainline churches usually reject that fundamentalist
view, focusing instead on the more moderate view, that, regardless of the
specific means of Jesus's conception, this story reminds us that God wanted
a relationship with humanity so much that God crossed the bounds of the
humanity-divinity divide to connect with us. Even if we do go as far as
arguing that the story is mythical, we need to remember what a myth is and
why this story still matters. Myths are not stories that are untrue, save for in
a factual sense; instead, myths provide deep truths that give a person and a
community meaning for living one's life. They are not superimposed upon

13

a culture by someone either from within or outside of that culture; rather, they come from within a culture, naturally, often spontaneously, as a way of trying to articulate a truth people can find no other words for.

If the story of the Virgin Birth, then, is a myth (and I won't ever say that something is *only* or *just* a myth, as that devalues the importance of myth), we need to see what the story is trying to tell us about God and the relationship between humanity and divinity. If we can see the truth at that end of the spectrum, it will help shape our thinking, no matter what we believe about the historical truth of the event. It might help us to remember at this point that Jewish readers (to whom the author of Matthew is writing) read stories without concern for their historical truth. It's not that they disbelieved such stories; instead, they could read a story on both an historical and metaphorical level at the same time. Those of us in the West have largely lost the ability to do so, as we are much more concerned about whether or not something is true in an historical sense, only, as if other stories have nothing to teach us.

That said, one way of looking at this passage is to look at Jesus's names. He has two of them, sort of. In the section of Isaiah the author of Matthew quotes, the person who fulfills this prophecy—Jesus, of course—shall be named Emmanuel, which means "God with us." This name sums up the importance of the incarnation, in that those who believe Jesus is God on Earth read this information completely literally. Again, one doesn't have to do so to still be moved by the idea that this birth reminds us of God's love for humanity and that God is involved and interested in the lives of each of us. God is not simply "with us" when Jesus walked the streets of Jerusalem or Capernaum, but God is with us because of the relationship we have with the divine, represented by the life of Jesus.

The passage from I John makes this idea clear, as the repeated emphasis on love as the manifestation of God shows. That author reminds us that, when we love, we are acting as God acts, that we are embodying God in the same way that Jesus did, that we are exhibiting God to the world, that we are carrying God with us everywhere we go and to everyone we meet, that we are helping others to see God as we have seen him in the life of Jesus and the lives of our Christian communities. The author tells us that "those who abide in love abide in God, and God abides in them." Jesus comes to bring love to all people, including those whom the first century Jewish leaders had forgotten, and we abide in love and in God when we practice that radical inclusivity that illustrates how God is with us.

Along the same lines, Jesus's name means some version of "God saves" (the Hebrew verb root literally means "rescue" or "deliver," but "saves" is how most scholars translate the meaning of the name). While the traditional reading of this passage is that God saves humanity from their sins through Jesus's life, death, and resurrection, there is more to this meaning than that. This focus on love and abiding in love by imitating Jesus shows us that God saves us from more than simply our original sinfulness. God saves us from our selfish behaviors that push us to ignore the poor or marginal; God saves us from a culture that tells we are nothing more than a consumer, put on this planet to purchase more and more until we die; God saves us from a political arena that benefits from dividing us from one another through the use of fear; God saves us from a life of alienation, as we can become one with others, not out of our own efforts, but through the love of God that defies all explanations, as does a story about a young woman giving birth to a baby boy who shows us that love.

Questions for Reflection or Discussion:

Where do we see "God with us" today, especially in acts of love and inclusivity?

What do we need saving from, and how does Jesus's life help show us ways toward that salvation?

Taking Action

Christmas Day

John 1:1–14
Isaiah 52:7–10

WHENEVER PEOPLE TALK ABOUT this passage from John, the idea of *logos* comes up on a regular basis. People want to lay out how the meaning of that Greek word is much richer than our English word *word*. They will describe *logos* as possibly meaning "ground," as in the very foundation of the world or God's agent in the world, among a whole host of other interpretations. Granted, translation works this way, as we often take a word from another language that has a rich connotation and sum it up in one English word that cannot contain all the nuances of the original. That's part of the problem with trying to read the Bible literally.

However, whenever I think of this passage, I think of a Call to Worship that one of my teenage friends wrote when I was either in high school or college. He had been taking Spanish for several years, and he had a copy of a Spanish New Testament. Instead of reading the opening passage of John in English, he started in Spanish, as he wanted to emphasize that word *word* in Spanish. Instead of using the Spanish word for *word*, the translators use the word *verbo*, which, as one might guess, means *verb*. Thus, one translation from Spanish to English would read, "In the beginning was the Verb, and Verb was with God, and the Verb was God."

Perhaps it's my English background speaking here, but I love this word choice. The English *word* certainly provides interesting interpretations, and *logos* is much closer to the intent of the author of John, but *verb* adds a layer that reminds me of who Jesus actually is and what's important in the gospels. *Verb* implies action, doing, which is how we usually describe it to students who are learning grammar. In fact, I often talk about passive voice in my classes, and I try to describe it as a problem that occurs when writers move the person or thing doing the acting after the verb that describes the action.

I should say that Jesus is certainly not exclusively about action, as he often took time away from the crowds to try to find solitude, and he encouraged his disciples to do the same. However, even in those moments of solitude, he is preparing for the action, the work he was focused on. He needed those times away from people to be able to actively care for others. Most of the time, though, we see Jesus in action, whether that's speaking to a crowd, eating with a wide variety of people, or healing those who are suffering.

However, this emphasis on action is not a means to perpetuate guilt, as I'm not trying to use this word choice as a way to tell people they're not doing enough. Instead, I want to separate dogma from praxis. Dogma is a set of beliefs that one has, while praxis is putting those beliefs into action, essentially embodying those beliefs in some way. This distinction is one the church has often overlooked, at least for much of its history.

Many churches now, and the larger church for centuries, focus on encouraging people to have the right beliefs. They want people to understand the trinity or be able to explain how Jesus's death on the cross leads to salvation through the idea of atonement. Some churches widen this approach out to social issues, where one needs to have the correct belief on abortion or same-sex marriage or euthanasia. In such situations, what distinguishes people as Christian is that they hold the correct set of beliefs. If people are in line with the rest of the church on this set of beliefs, then they must be Christians.

This approach doesn't really work with how the gospel writers present Jesus, however. Jesus doesn't come with a new set of stone tables to replace the Ten Commandments; instead, he comes to act out the life he wants those who follow him to emulate. Even when he does provide instructions on how to live (such as the Sermon on the Mount or the two great commandments), they are often quite vague. Telling people to love their neighbors isn't all that helpful on a day-to-day basis, as we often find ourselves in situations where loving someone feels much like denying them what they actually want. The parables seemingly make this easier, if we think of parables like the Good Samaritan or the Prodigal Son, but there are many other parables that simply leave us more confused than when we started.

Rather than emphasizing the right beliefs, Jesus emphasizes the right actions. When he is eating with a Pharisee, he praises the woman who is using her tears and hair to wash his feet. He doesn't ask her what she believes; he simply observes what she is doing, concluding from that action the type of love she has. When people come to be healed, he often responds by saying that their faith has healed them, as it was not their dogma that led to their healing, but their willingness to step out in faith.

This passage from John comes on Christmas Day, a day where we talk about the incarnation, the coming of Jesus as a human. We spend a good deal of time arguing over exactly what that means (as the church has for hundreds of years; see the Nicene Creed for evidence), as we think we need the correct belief about who or what Jesus is. Jesus seems to think praxis is much more important, that we need to spend our time loving one another, caring for those on the margins, reaching out to those whom society has ignored. If we do those actions, those verbs, our dogma won't matter, as we'll be living as Jesus did, as he wants us to do.

Questions for Reflection or Discussion:

What are beliefs the church has emphasized for years that might distract us from action?

Where are places—either in the Bible or our lives—where we see people who might not have the orthodox or approved dogma acting out God's love?

Border Crossing

First Sunday After Christmas

Matthew 2:13–23
Isaiah 63:7–14

THERE HAS BEEN A great deal of discussion about immigration, migrants, and refugees recently. Then again, there is always significant amounts of discussion around these issues, as they are issues the world and, specifically, America have struggled with almost as long as we have existed as a country. With the recent refugee crisis in Europe, stemming from the violence in the Middle East, we have become even more focused on the issue. That discussion is in addition to the normal discussion Americans have about immigration from Mexico and Latin America. All of these events become even more tension-filled now that Americans elected Donald Trump as President. Whether it's his comments from the election when he talked about Mexicans as "rapists," among other insults, or his attempt to ban travel from Muslim-majority countries, our ability to talk about these issues has become even more difficult.

Throughout the decades in America, what has remained constant in this discussion is the rhetoric surrounding the issue, with the only change coming in who we vilify at the time. Whether it's the Irish coming over carrying their Catholicism, which threatened to disrupt the Protestant majority, or Jews fleeing the Third Reich, but bringing their threatening clothing and odd-seeming beliefs (not to mention their propensity to keep to themselves), or Muslims with women wearing the hijab and their supposed threats of terrorism, those who wish to keep others out focus only on our differences, those parts of their lives Americans don't take the time to understand. The rhetoric is one of fear and hate.

Unfortunately, for much of American history, significant parts of the church have been at the forefront of such rhetoric, often quoting parts of the Old Testament about keeping separate from others or the threats of intermarriage as justification for why we should keep America as a Christian (which is really code for white, evangelical, and Protestant) nation. That has begun to shift in recent years, as more and more churches become involved in refugee resettlement, but the years of accretion have laid a foundation of distrust and fear and hate, which churches must intentionally combat, as the church has been responsible for its creation.

This story about Jesus, then, comes at the right time, as Jesus fits so many of these categories. Jesus fits the definition of a migrant, according to the *Oxford English Dictionary*: "A person who moves temporarily or seasonally from place to place." Jesus also fits the definition of a refugee: "A person who has been forced to leave his or her home and seek refuge elsewhere, esp. in a foreign country, from war, religious persecution, political troubles, the effects of a natural disaster, etc.; a displaced person." In fact, if we focus on the part of the definition that centers around religious persecution and/ or political troubles, Jesus seems the quintessential refugee.

Jesus is fleeing genocide, caused by his appearance (and the belief that he is the long-expected Messiah, leading to the religious persecution), the slaughter of the innocents, as many people often refer to this passage. Joseph has to take his family to Egypt to keep them alive, then he has to go to Nazareth rather than Bethlehem, as Joseph is afraid to return his family to where they have been living for at least two years (based on the age of the children Herod kills) and possibly longer. In the gospel of Matthew's account, Joseph and Mary didn't come from Nazareth down to Bethlehem for the census; that only shows up in the gospel of Luke. Instead, it sounds as if Joseph and Mary have always been living in Bethlehem. Thus, Nazareth becomes the place that takes in the refugee family, as they have had to resettle there. Jesus, then, spends the first three or so years of his life being forcibly relocated from Bethlehem to Egypt, then to Nazareth where the family has to begin all over again, as refugees today do. Joseph and Mary, though, are at least able to resettle in a place where they know the language, religion, and culture, unlike so many refugees today.

There is never any evidence that they struggle from this resettlement, but we also don't have any information about the next ten or so years of Jesus's life in any of the gospels. We do know that Joseph disappears, which would have made their life more difficult if he died or for some other reason was taken away from the family.

The passage from Isaiah draws on God's salvation for the people of Israel when they were refugees, when they were fleeing Egypt, as well, and moving to what would become Israel. What is interesting to note, though, is what happens after they arrive. The first half of this passage talks about all that God has done for the Israelites, commenting, "Surely they are my people, children who will not deal falsely." The author of Isaiah clearly lays out the idea that people who have received such grace and salvation will never cease to appreciate such goodness in their life. The second half of the passage makes it clear that they have stopped remembering what God has done, though it ends with hope that such a view of the world will change.

The same pattern is true when we talk about how Americans have treated those who have come after us. All of us (save for those American Indians among us) came from immigrants, many as migrants and refugees, fleeing persecution. Our ancestors came here and set themselves up in new lives, working to provide for their children and grandchildren. Now that we are established, though, we turn against those who might come after us, treating them as the Other, even as our ancestors were so treated. The only hope we have is to see them all as Jesus, as ourselves, and to love them accordingly. Only then will we be able to say, as the end of the passage from Isaiah does, "Thus you led your people, to make for yourself a glorious name."

Questions for Reflection or Discussion:

How should we as churches and as Christians help with the refugee crisis?

What can the church do to shift the immigration debate towards one of love?

Tipping Points
The Feast of the Epiphany

Matthew 2:1–12
Ephesians 3:1–12

T HE LECTIONARY SELECTIONS ARE clearly trying to guide an interpretation of the passage from the gospel of Matthew for Epiphany. With the inclusion of Galatians talking about the Gentiles, the predominant way of reading the arrival of the Magi is to talk about how Jesus's coming broadens God's message out from the Jews to the inclusion of the Gentiles. From there, it makes sense to talk about how Jesus's arrival and ministry is one that centers around crossing boundaries or barriers. Now that God's love is clearly available to all (there are Old Testament passages that also state that it is, but we tend to ignore those to make a clear divide between Old Testament exclusion and Jesus's New Testament inclusion), Jesus serves as a representative of that widening.

I don't want to diminish such a reading, as Jesus's life and ministry clearly reflect this idea. Whether it was women or tax collectors or Samaritans or Pharisees or Romans or prostitutes, Jesus reached out to everyone he encountered, no matter their ethnicity or religious beliefs or gender or status in society. Jesus's life exemplifies how we, too, should not let barriers keep us from truly loving our neighbors, no matter who they and we are. There are plenty of passages that illustrate that idea.

What the story of the arrival of the Magi should also illustrate is the power that dominates our world, but also how that power is much more fragile than we imagine. When the wise men from the East arrive and stop to ask King Herod where the child who "has been born King of the Jews" is, the text reads, "When King Herod heard this, he was frightened, and all Jerusalem with him . . . " Here is one of the most powerful people in the area, still under the dominion of Rome, certainly, but with almost unchecked power, and he is frightened by these wise men who have come into his country looking for a child, whom they say will be the King of the Jews.

That fear will ultimately lead Herod to kill all of the children he believes could possibly be the one the wise men tell him about, and it leads him to mislead the wise men here. He is so unsure of his power that he becomes so shaken by the simple arrival of a child that he is willing to slaughter countless children. We typically don't think of power in this way. Instead, we think of those who are so secure in their positions that they have no worries, that their lives are ones of ease and comfort.

However, what those in power know (and what those of us not in those positions often forget) is how precarious that power actually is. They have seen people who have tried, as they did, to move up those levels only to be denied, whether through demotions, exile, or even death. These successful people were often the ones doing the demoting, exiling, or killing, in fact. Given that they know how easily they could dispose of other people, they also know how tenuous their hold on their position is. If they could do these horrific actions to someone else, then someone could just as easily remove them in one of these ways.

Rather than provide us with discouragement about the evils of humanity (though we should certainly remember that truth), we should draw hope from this story, as there are other ways of removing people of power, even by those of us who seemingly have little in our society. The Herods of this world must not only worry about those whom they have wronged on their way up or the ones who will come after them, trying to supplant them. They must also worry about the people they supposedly have power over, as people will only remain in those positions for a certain amount of time. If history teaches us anything, it shows us that people—when gathered together for a common cause against oppression—can overthrow those in power.

The problem the powerless have is that the powerful seem invulnerable, but they only seem that way until they no longer do. For those who grew up during the Cold War, the Berlin Wall seemed impregnable until it was torn down. For those who suffered through years of oppression via Jim Crow laws, those rules seemed immovable until they weren't. For those in wheelchairs or blind, the obstacles that prevented them from entering buildings and jobs seemed insurmountable until they were no longer there. For those who wanted to marry their partners of the same sex, the laws that kept them from doing so seemed to be set in stone until the Supreme Court said otherwise.

Of course, we all know that all of these groups (and others) still suffer in our society. People on the LGBTQ spectrum still face obvious and subtle discrimination, as do People of Color and women and immigrants, among others. However, throughout the twentieth and into the twenty-first century, groups of those who seem to have no power in society say that they will not accept such treatment any longer. They stand up to the people in power, and they make changes in society.

Across the world, from the Arab Spring to movements for democracy in Africa to protests in Russia to people marching in America, people without obvious power stand up to those who clearly have it, and they change the world. Herod knew that one child born in Bethlehem, whom these wise men had dubbed the King of the Jews, could depose him. He was wrong, on a literal level, as he died long before Jesus grew up, but he was right where it counted. Herod's type of power will always lose out to the power of unconditional love that Jesus preached. Herod knew how shaky his position was. Those of us who wish to see justice in the world must always remember that, too.

Questions for Reflection or Discussion:

Where are places where people have overthrown power, especially when it appeared impossible or highly unlikely they could do so?

Where are places people still need to overthrow power, even when it looks impossible to do so?

Good News

First Sunday After the Epiphany

Luke 3:15–22 (also Matthew 3:13–21 and Mark 1:4–11)
Isaiah 42:1–9

THE THREE GOSPEL ACCOUNTS of Jesus's baptism are largely the same, at least in terms of the general outline: John the Baptist is preaching, Jesus shows up, and John baptizes him. There are a variety of differences, ranging from minor word choice changes to something as obvious as the switch in point of view in the comments from the voice from heaven (switching from third person in Matthew to second person in Mark and Luke). The author of Luke, though, uses a phrase that neither of the other two authors use: "good news." We normally wouldn't be surprised to see this phrase in one of the gospel accounts, as it's a phrase we use in our churches on a regular basis, and we generally agree on what we mean by it.

In the passage from Luke, though, it's used at a place and in a way that seems rather odd. Rather than signifying some sort of salvation, it is related more to judgment. John tells the crowd that Jesus is coming to "clear his threshing-floor" and that he will burn the chaff "with unquenchable fire." That doesn't sound like the type of good news we talk about today. If one is the wheat, they might see it as good news, but the image of some sort of eternal punishment sounds more like the fire and brimstone sermons many of us have heard.

The church has used the phrase "good news" in this way far too many times in our long history, essentially trying to portray the eternal suffering that one will suffer without God in an attempt to force people into believing their particular brand of salvation. The "good news" in such a sermon is that one doesn't have to endure that eternal suffering, that God has provided a way out of that eternity and into one with Jesus and the other Christians. My friends and I used to joke that they (or we, if we're honest) were trying to scare the hell out of people. The only reason anyone needed any type of salvation was to avoid this suffering that would come if they didn't choose to accept Jesus as their Lord and Savior. Luke's addition of "and fire" after "Holy Spirit," explaining what Jesus would baptize believers with reinforces such an idea.

Perhaps, though, "good news" doesn't refer to that idea of suffering, as it's connected to the word "exhortations." John is encouraging those who have come to hear him, not condemning them. Granted, he is quite clear about what will happen to the chaff, but he also seems to believe that people will follow Jesus. He tells them that Jesus, the one to come after him, "will baptize [them] with the Holy Spirit," implying that they will want that baptism. He seems to be saying that they will be so drawn to Jesus that they will want Jesus to baptize them with the Holy Spirit and fire. In fact, near the end of the passage, Luke's author says, "Now when all the people were baptized . . . " The author isn't arguing that everyone who heard John was baptized, but people are clearly coming to hear John and responding to his "good news."

That "good news" becomes clear once John baptizes Jesus and the voice from heaven speaks. People usually discuss this voice from heaven in one of two ways. Either they focus on the fact that it clearly shows that Jesus is God's son or they talk about the trinity, given that all three members are in one place at the same time (assuming the voice from heaven is God). Thus, many people assume the good news here is that Jesus is God's son.

However, there is another part of that voice from heaven's comment that gives us more reason to see good news in the beginning of Jesus's ministry. At the end of the voice from heaven's comments, it says, "with you I am well pleased." Such a statement shouldn't be surprising, given that the voice from heaven is talking about Jesus. What's interesting, though, is when such a statement appears in Jesus's life. If Jesus's mission is to come to Earth, provide a model for how people should live, and save them from their sins by dying on the cross, there is no reason for God to be well pleased with Jesus at this point, as Jesus hasn't done anything besides come to Earth (that we're aware of).

Instead, God makes this comment to Jesus because God is well pleased with Jesus for simply being, not because Jesus has done anything to earn God's pleasure. God is well pleased because Jesus is God's son. God is well pleased because Jesus is God's beloved. In the same way, God is well pleased with us, not because of what we have accomplished or because of what we hope to accomplish, but merely because we are children of God. We are God's beloved; thus, God is well pleased with us. God loves Jesus just as he is; in the same way, God loves us just as we are. Jesus's entire life acts out this single principle. The passage in Isaiah says that God's servant is one in whom God's soul delights. We are people in whom God delights.

If that passage in Isaiah is describing Jesus or simply any of God's servants, there is an emphasis on justice, as the author mentions it three times in just a few verses. God's servant will bring justice to the nations or to the Earth simply by behaving as God behaves. God loves Jesus and us just as he and we are. Those of us who claim to be in God and of God should do the same. Such an approach is the way to bring justice to this world, by loving others simply for being and for being who they are. That is the good news John and Jesus bring.

Questions for Reflection or Discussion:

Where and how have you seen the phrase "good news" used and misused?

What difference does it make in our lives when we shift from seeing God's love as something we earn to something freely given?

Hearing the Call

Second Sunday After the Epiphany

John 1:43–51
I Samuel 3:1–10

T HE READINGS FOR THE Second Sunday after the Epiphany present a
particular problem to many progressive Christians, as many of us are
uncomfortable when we talk about God's call. The language itself causes
a problem, as many people would not want to say, even in church, that
God had called them to something. That type of speech is usually indica-
tive of the more Pentecostal churches, or at least the evangelical part of
the faith. We especially wouldn't want to stand up and church and make a
grand declaration about how God had called us to do something dramatic,
maybe leave our jobs and pursue some sort of ministry opportunity. Unfortunately, we don't have any language to talk about any time we do feel
God is encouraging us to do something (assuming we feel God does act in
that manner).

Both of these passages, then, can make twenty-first century Christians feel as if the Bible has nothing to say to us. Samuel is literally called
by God, so much so that he is confused as to whose voice he's hearing,
leading him to go to Eli (three times, no less, as neither Samuel nor Eli
seem quick to pick up on the fact that Samuel is hearing from God). Jesus
also is calling disciples to him at the beginning of his ministry, which goes
more smoothly. He simply tells Philip to follow him, and Philip does (most
scholars believe that Jesus had been teaching for some time before actually
encouraging people to be his disciples, but note that what we do when we
talk this way is lessen the dramatic nature of that call, which is the part that
bothers us the most). Nathanael might be a more difficult disciple, but Jesus

simply tells him a couple of facts, one of which Jesus should not have been able to know, and he decides to leave everything to follow Jesus, as well.

It is not the fact that Samuel or Philip or Nathanael decide to pursue God or Jesus in these passages, as any of us who profess to be Christian would say that we do the same. What does bother us is that there seems to be no reflection, no thought put into the process. Instead, God or Jesus simply speaks or appears, and the people respond. We would take time to think through the matter today, perhaps form a committee to help us decide if we were really hearing from God or not, explore all of our options, then make a reasoned and well-researched choice. When we hear from God (if we even use that terminology), we hear over the course of weeks or months or even years.

Part of our reluctance to embrace these stories is that we don't want God to enter our lives in such a dramatic fashion. We want to be certain we are doing what is right, that we have done our due diligence, as we often say, before we take action. We want to have plans in place—even back-up plans in case our primary plan doesn't work—so there are no surprises once we make the choice. We want to *know* rather than simply to believe that God is calling us into some major decision.

A larger part of our hesitation, though, is that we just don't believe God truly calls us today, or at least not in any way that is similar to these two passages. We don't expect to be lying in bed and hear the voice of God calling to us (and calling us by name). We don't believe we will be outside under a tree and Jesus will want us to follow him. These are stories from a time that has long since passed, and we have work to be done. Even if God were to speak in this way, we wouldn't hear.

However, the combination of these stories might show us a way that God does, in fact, still speak to us, does still call us to difficult work, even in rather dramatic fashion. Samuel's story is the one we have the most difficulty with, as most of us go through life never hearing God's voice calling our name in the dark of night. However, we should note that it is Eli who helps him understand that God is speaking to him, even telling him what to say. In the account from John, the author of that gospel shows Philip going to talk to Nathanael, even having to convince him to come and see Jesus, as Nathanael is the quintessential skeptic.

Perhaps one of the major ways we hear from God in our world (and have always heard from God) is through other people, sometimes even those committees I slightly mocked earlier. We need to see the Philips and Elis of our lives who are trying to get us to listen, to hear whatever it is

God wants us to do with our lives. They are ministers, certainly, but, more often, they are friends or family members or co-workers or people we meet once at a party or sporting event or on the bus or subway. If we are open to hearing the voice of God, we should listen to their encouraging us to be this or do that or go there and have the courage to act upon those comments.

We might not hear God call our names at night or see Jesus underneath a tree, but the community we find in one another often speaks the words of God to us when we're willing to hear. God might be trying to tell us about a great work we can do in the world, but we're unable to hear because we read stories about Philip and Nathanael and Samuel and Eli, and we think God doesn't talk to us like that. God speaks in ways we can hear in a world very different than the one we read about, but God is still speaking, nonetheless.

Questions for Reflection or Discussion:

When or how have you felt God calling or speaking to you throughout your life?

What are some times when you have acted more on faith than on well thought-out plans?

Exceptionalism

Third Sunday After the Epiphany

Luke 4:16–30
Jonah 3:1–5, 10

WHILE THE GOSPEL OF John begins with the wedding at Cana as Jesus's first public appearance, the author of Luke places Jesus's appearance in the synagogue at Nazareth at the beginning of Jesus's ministry. It's clear, even from the text, that this account isn't actually Jesus's first appearance, as he makes reference to the Nazarenes having heard what he did in Capernaum. For the author of Luke, though, this event is important enough that he wanted to use it immediately after Jesus's time in the wilderness, wanted to set up Jesus's ministry with it.

Part of that inclination probably comes from Jesus's reading from Isaiah, as it clearly echoes Mary's Magnificat that the author of Luke uses in the first chapter. There is a strong emphasis on a reversal of the status quo, a turning-upside-down of the world as it currently stands in Jesus's reading, which will become a trend in the gospel of Luke. Jesus's dramatic declaration that this scripture "has been fulfilled in [their] hearing" makes clear what this gospel will focus on.

However, it is not just this opening quote from Isaiah that sets a tone for the gospel of Luke. After Jesus reads that scripture and makes his declaration, people receive him warmly; they are "amazed at the gracious words that came from his mouth" and talk about his being "Joseph's son." In fact, it's not clear why Jesus reacts to those comments by criticizing the Nazarenes and why he believes they do not (or will not) accept him. One possibility comes from their mentioning his being Joseph's son, though, as they seem rather proud of that fact. One reading of this part of the story is that they are trying to claim him as their own, that they want to emphasize the fact that he's one of them.

The rest of this passage certainly supports such a reading, as Jesus wants to make it clear to those in the synagogue that he has not come solely for the Israelites. He spends the rest of his time in the synagogue criticizing any focus on Israel as special, in fact. He reminds them that God has provided for surrounding countries in the past, even while not supporting Israel. He references Elijah and Elisha, two of the most important prophets, as if he is setting himself in their lineage. It's easy to see that the author of this gospel simply wants to remind people that Jesus has come for the Gentiles as well as the Jews, but this passage goes well beyond that to show not just a broadening of Jesus's message, but times where God ignored the needs of Israel.

Jesus, though, isn't trying to say his ministry is not for the Jews, as his actions throughout this and the other gospels clearly show that it is. Instead, he wants to remind them that they are not exceptional, that they are part of an entire world that God loves and that Jesus will serve, so he draws on two well-known examples to do so. He is making it clear that the Messiah they expected—the one who would overthrow Rome and create a new Israel—is not who he will be. Instead, he will heal and feed everyone who needs healing and feeding, no matter where they come from or who they are.

The people of Nineveh from Jonah serve as a contrast to the Israelites in Luke, as they hear Jonah's message, and they immediately repent. Where the Israelites are angry that Jesus has pointed out their shortcomings and react with violence, the Ninevites respond with repentance, proclaiming a fast and putting on sackcloth. These two responses definitely serve as examples of how individuals can respond, but they also illustrate how we talk and think about countries, as well.

On a regular basis, people in the public sphere have a debate about whether or not America is a "Christian nation." Sometimes, that discussion comes around Christmas when there is a debate about whether people in retail or in service industries should wish people a Merry Christmas or Happy Holidays. Politicians often use America's supposed Christian heritage when they are running for office or trying to pass bills that represent their view of Christianity (and of America), whether that be issues such as abortion and same-sex marriage or more directly faith-based legislation, such as prayer in schools.

All too often, Christian Americans respond as the Israelites, though, not as the Ninevites, taking any criticism of the way they blend their national and Christian identities as an attack on what they perceive to be the very foundations of both. While it doesn't lead to anyone threatening to throw someone over a cliff, such discussions often lead to one attack after another on the other side, often labeling the other side as anti-American or anti-Christian or both. The cynical response to such debates is to see people as using both patriotism and faith as means to an end, not as the true motivating factor.

What can help Americans be both Americans and Christians, though, is the passage from Isaiah Jesus begins with. The reversal Jesus lays out should remind us all that God's idea of power and strength doesn't come from a strong political process or military might or even a robust democracy. Instead, God's idea of power and strength comes from caring for those who are least able to take care of themselves. Being exceptional has nothing to do with where we are born or what our nationality is or even what those national roots are; it has everything to do with turning the world upside down, being willing to put others ahead of us. The only way to be exceptional in God's kingdom is to care for the poor and the blind and the captives and the oppressed; that is how one proclaims the year of the Lord's favor.

Questions for Reflection or Discussion:

Who or where are groups of people the church often ignores or even actively excludes? How can we do better at including them?

How can we balance political involvement with our faith, especially as we guard against letting our politics dictate our faith? How can we make sure we're Christians first, then Americans (or whatever nationality we might be) only after that?

Not Pie in the Sky By and By

Fourth Sunday After the Epiphany

Matthew 5:1–12
Micah 6:1–8

THE BEATITUDES ARE A troublesome passage, not so much because of what they say, but because of how people have used them over the years. Because almost all of them end with a supposed reward that is set in the future, people use them to talk about what the people who fulfill these descriptions will receive not now, but in heaven (or at least some sort of distant future). Slave owners often used such verses, even editing them, to remind slaves that they should be meek or that, if they hunger and thirst now (note the omission), they will be filled when they are ultimately in heaven, where they will be because they are meek.

Along the same lines, men used this passage against women for centuries, and some still do. In the same way the slave owners used such verses for control, the men have and do, as well. They, too, might edit out parts to remind women that they didn't need money, as the poor will receive the kingdom of heaven. As with the slave owners, they also forced women to be meek, which they interpreted as doing whatever the man (often the husband) said the woman should do.

While talking about these ideas in this way, they reminded (or remind) the slaves or women that "blessed" doesn't really mean "blessed"; instead, the better translation is "happy," a point preachers continue to emphasize. For the slave owners and men, then, it was clear that those whom they were oppressing should not only be meek or poor or hungry or thirsty; they should be happy to be in that state. Doing otherwise was against the will of God. These verses became an instrument of control, coercion, and oppression instead of providing the liberation Jesus intended.

The focus on the future, though, still hampers how we read this passage. We still talk about how those who suffer in some way here on Earth will receive some sort of future reward, whether we accept the traditional idea of heaven or have some other idea. Such a view does provide comfort to those who are going through difficult times, as they can remember that, though they mourn now, they will one day receive comfort. Many people who have had family members or friends die use such an interpretation to help them get through one of the most difficult times of their lives.

However, such an approach that puts any reward in the future deprives us of the joy (which is different from happiness) we should seek and provide to one another right now, not in some distant future. We often interpret these verses in a way that causes them to read like this: "Blessed are those who mourn, for God will comfort them in heaven." That reading, though, makes two assumptions that shift our reading in unfortunate ways. It implies God will do the comforting, and that comforting will happen in heaven. Given its construction, though, one could also read the verse as, "Blessed are those who mourn, for others will comfort them when they do mourn." It's still in the future, but a much more conceivable future, a future almost all of us will experience when we suffer some loss that causes us to mourn.

Such a reading not only shifts the emphasis from some distant future life to our time here on Earth, it also points out that we have communities of people—ideally, the church—who will surround us and help us through those awful times in our lives. Rather than waiting for comfort from God in heaven, we can receive comfort from one another here, in our present lives. If we truly work for righteousness, we will see it come to fruition, perhaps in small ways, but we will see it, nonetheless. If we are merciful people, others will be merciful to us. If we are pure in heart, we will see God, not in some future life, but here and now.

In fact, if we look at the opening of Jesus's list of blessings, we see that it is not written in a future tense at all, but in the clear present. If we are poor in spirit, we will have the kingdom of God, not sometime in the future, but now: "theirs *is* the kingdom of heaven." If we put others ahead of ourselves, if we work for justice and righteousness, if we provide mercy, then we will create the kingdom of heaven on Earth for others and for ourselves. We're not doing such actions to earn our place in a future heaven where we will reap some reward; we're doing those actions to show love to one another, as that's how we create the kingdom of heaven.

Of course, such an approach shifts the responsibility from God to us. We can no longer tell people that God will comfort them at some point, as God is calling us to comfort them ourselves. We must be the ones who work for justice and righteousness now, rather than waiting on some divine reckoning in the future to bring any sort of leveling to the inequalities of the world. We must be the peacemakers, working to end all strife, whether the wars that continue to kill and displace the innocent or the battles we fight in our office hallways or in ourselves.

The end of the passage from Micah sums up what the beatitudes lay out as the way to establish the kingdom of God: we are required to do justice, love kindness, and walk humbly with God. We must hunger and thirst for righteousness, be merciful, and be poor in spirit. We must not put off such actions until some future time; we must not shift the responsibility to God. Instead, we must work for the kingdom here and now, for everyone, in every way we can. Only then will we receive, not some superficial happiness, but true joy. At that point, we'll all be blessed.

Questions for Reflection or Discussion:

What are some things that prevent us from experiencing the kingdom here on earth?

How can we take on more of the responsibility for justice and righteousness, rather than shifting that responsibility to God?

Hide It Under a Bushel? No!

Fifth Sunday After the Epiphany

Matthew 5:13–20
Isaiah 58:3–9a

F OR THOSE OF US who grew up in the church, reading the passage about being the light of the world and letting that light shine almost always reminds us of the song we sang when we were younger. We had the hand motions to go along with letting our light shine and not hiding it under a bushel, yelling out "no!" when we asked the question about hiding it under a bushel (as if we knew what that was). We didn't understand much about that song, if we're honest, but it must have reinforced, at least for the adults, the idea that we would not be ashamed of being a Christian.

We almost never talk about what being the light of the world means now, preferring to talk about other parts of this passage, especially the salt. There have been so many sermons about salt, many of us feel like experts on the subject. We've heard all about how salt is a preservative or how it adds flavor to life (often connected to living life abundantly) or how important it was for ancient Israelites. Ironically, people often overlook the light.

Part of the hesitation in talking about that part of the passage from Matthew is the last part of the section on the light, where Jesus talks about "good works," stating that they should "shine before" others. Such wording goes against almost everything else we teach in the church. We tell people about grace and about how God loves us, not because of what we do, but because we are God's creation. We explain that we shouldn't try to earn our way to God's love through doing what we often call "good works." We say that we shouldn't advertise the work we do, that we should love each other in meaningful ways, but always without attracting anyone's notice.

We should certainly not draw attention to whatever good we are doing for one another. Yet here we have Jesus clearly stating that we should let our "light shine before others, so that they may see [our] good works."

Jesus, though, makes it clear where the glory for those good works should go, as what we do should not point to our goodness, but to the goodness of God. While this idea is true, it also leads to the belittling of others' work and talents. Too often in the church, we praise other people for the hard work they have put into something—a musical performance, cleaning the church kitchen, preparing meals for those who would go hungry otherwise—and they quickly demure, as they want to give the praise to God. This view of our work has led to people's lowering their view of their self-worth, and, unfortunately, it often leads to a hierarchy of abilities or work in the church, as if God values some people more because they do or don't do certain parts of the church's calling. That type of thinking leads to the true downside of celebrating good works.

Defining what our light actually is, though, might help deal with this passage, as we often leave the key idea here vague, as if we are still children singing that song without truly understanding it. The rest of the passage shows Jesus talking about the law and the prophets, about how he has come not to abolish them, but to fulfill them. The law and the prophets center on how we treat God and how we treat one another (becoming Jesus's two commandments). Whether we're talking about the Torah, where God lays out clear ideas for how to live in community, or the prophets, where they admonish the Israelites when they fall short of God's ideals for living with one another, the overriding idea of the law and the prophets is about experiencing true communion with each other because God loves us all and wishes us to share that love with everyone we encounter.

If Jesus is the light of the world, and Jesus is the epitome of that love, then so, too, has God called us to be that love in the world. That love is what we should show to anyone and everyone, not hiding it under a bushel. We should let our love shine before others, so that they will give glory to God, as such love could only come from one's connection with the divine, not from any mere human love.

The passage from Isaiah (one of those prophets Jesus has come to fulfill) makes this connection between light and love even clearer. After beginning with a question from the Israelites about why God does not see their fasts, Isaiah's response, speaking in the voice of God, is that their fasts are self-serving and lead to fights among themselves. Unlike Jesus's admonition in the passage from Matthew, the Israelites here are trying to let their personal lights shine, wanting to receive the glory themselves, which leads to strife in the community.

Isaiah then reminds them of what God values, which goes well beyond not eating food. Instead, God wants them to fight injustice and oppression, to share food with the hungry and welcome the homeless, to clothe the naked and support their families. Then, the author of Isaiah says their "light shall break forth from the dawn." God wants the Israelites and God wants us to speak out for those whom society has deprived of a voice, to feed those who are hungry, to provide shelter for those who need it, to do whatever we can to help whoever is around us and suffering.

Thus, whenever we support those whom society oppresses because of their race or sexuality or ability or gender, we let our lights shine. Whenever we give food or drink to the hungry, we let our lights shine. Whenever we stand up to a government that tries to deprive people of their basic rights and liberties, we let our lights shine. Whenever we forgive the person down the hall or down the street for how they have wronged us, we let our lights shine. We do all of these actions, not because we're perfect, but because God loves us all, and all of these acts point toward that love. There's no bushel that can hide such a love.

Questions for Reflection or Discussion:

What are some ways we can be light in our world today?

Where are places we hide light away, put it under a bushel? And why do we do so?

Are We Sure We Want Transformation?

Sixth Sunday After the Epiphany

Luke 6:17–26
Jeremiah 17:5–8

WHENEVER WE TALK ABOUT the beatitudes or the sermon on the mount, we're almost always talking about the version found in the gospel of Matthew. The version from the gospel of Luke, which people usually refer to as the sermon on the plain, given that Jesus clearly stands on a "level place," doesn't receive the same discussion. That lack of interest might be for practical reasons, in that the version from Matthew is much longer and covers a wider range of topics. Also, the list of beatitudes in the sermon on the mount is longer and more detailed; not surprisingly, it has become the one people both inside and outside of Christianity seem more interested in.

There might be another reason for the lack of interest in the sermon on the plain, though. Not only are these beatitudes shorter, they're also much more focused on tangible poverty. While the version from Matthew talks about people who are poor in spirit, the gospel of Luke talks about people who are poor. The sermon on the mount discusses those who hunger and thirst for righteousness, while the sermon on the plain is interested in people who are hungry. The longer version seems to provide us with more of an excuse not to do anything practical in this world. We can say we are working to help make the world more just by focusing on righteousness or people's spirits, more abstract ideas. This passage, though, makes it clear that the people who are poor or hungry on a literal, concrete level are the ones we should be interested in.

Such an approach is in keeping with the gospel of Luke, as this author is clearly concerned about those on the margins of society. He emphasizes women and Gentiles, the prostitutes and tax collectors, and, as here, the lower classes, those whom the religious establishment largely ignored. Mary's Magnificat comes in the opening chapter and sounds strikingly similar to this sermon on the plain, so it seems Jesus paid attention to his mother's prophetic utterings about the kingdom of God and is sharing those ideas with a larger audience.

One other major difference between the sermon on the mount and the one on the plain is that this version includes woes in addition to blessings. Those woes are also clearly focused on material success, as Jesus makes it clear what the rich and the full and the laughing can expect in the future. They should enjoy what they have now, as they're not going to have those material possessions or full stomachs in the future. This part might be another clear reason why we tend to ignore the gospel of Luke's portrayal of this sermon.

We often work diligently in the American church to avoid talking about wealth. We are certainly willing to discuss money, especially when it comes to finding ways to helping the poor, and we will definitely talk about stewardship to the church. Even there, though, we tend to talk about time and talents, in addition to money, mainly to avoid creating guilt for those without much money. We simply assume those of us who have money can interpret what we mean, and those of us who have spent any amount of time in the church definitely do so.

We ignore the numerous passages like this one where Jesus (or God in the Old Testament) talks explicitly about what the wealthy can expect in the future. We immediately find ways to explain away whatever the literal meaning of the passage is, finding refuge in some sort of metaphorical reading. We try to connect this passage with the sermon on the mount and argue that Jesus is not really discussing financial wealth here or literal hunger, but that he is talking about some spiritual truth that we're simply having trouble discerning. Almost no one stands up and preaches on this passage and says quite simply that Jesus makes it clear that the wealthy and the full and the laughing will one day not be any of those.

The reason we don't talk about wealth is obvious: many of us are wealthy. Even those of us who are at the bottom end of middle class still have a great deal of wealth compared to the poorest in our society, not to mention throughout the world. We have possessions people fifty years ago would have defined as luxuries, whether that's televisions or smart phones or home internet access or video games or multiple cars. On average, we eat out multiple times a week instead of making all of our meals at home, and we raise almost none of our food. We think nothing of driving twenty to thirty miles for activities or even to attend church, ignoring the gas we are using in the process (not to mention the effect on the environment).

Many of us in progressive churches, though, are not at the lower end of the middle class, and we should be honest about that. Financially, on average, members of progressive churches do quite well. Thus, we tend to avoid these passages because they make us uncomfortable. We are the people Jesus is speaking to here, and his words are not comforting. We like Mary's Magnificat because it talks about the powerful, and we don't feel that we have power in that way. Here, though, Jesus talks about what we do have, and we don't like it.

It's easy to talk about turning a world upside down or transforming the world until we realize what many of us will have to give up in that process. In Flannery O'Connor's story, "Revelation," Mrs. Turpin (a woman who consistently ranks people in society to make sure of her place above blacks and poor whites) has a vision of this reversal, and she cries out, "Put that bottom rail on top. There'll still be a top and bottom!" Jesus is not arguing for that result; rather, he's arguing for radical inclusivity and equality, and that means most of us will have to give up what we have. If I want other people to have more of something—food, money, power, shelter—I will have to give up some of each of those. If I want people to have more equality, I will have to give up my privilege. If I want those who are different than I am, whether in sexual orientation or gender identity or ability, to live the life I do, one where they don't have to worry about their safety in all the meanings of that word, I will have to give up some of what I have, and that reality, when I'm honest, worries me.

The only way we can take such a radical step is to take the approach from Jeremiah's prophecies. The author reminds us that those who trust in other people or in our strength will have no lasting roots and will wither away, while those who trust in the Lord will be like the tree planted by water with roots that spread out and give it life. As long as we trust in wealth, in our own ability to provide for ourselves, we will lead empty lives. It is only when we are willing to take the privilege we have, as well as the financial wealth, and joyfully give to those who don't have, trusting that God will provide, that we will be truly content and that we will see a greater glimpse of the kingdom.

Questions for Reflection or Discussion:

What are other reasons passages such as the one from the gospel of Luke make us nervous?

What are areas where those of us with something need to find ways to give it away? How do we go about doing so?

It's Just That Simple

Seventh Sunday After the Epiphany

Luke 6:27–38 (see also Matthew 5:38–48)
Leviticus 19:1–2, 9–18

MOST OF WHAT WE learn in the church, whether in worship or in some sort of Christian education program, is not actually something we didn't already know. That's especially true for people who grew up in the church, but it's also true for those who came in as adults. The reason is simple: there's just not much to Christianity. We spend much of our time complicating the simple ideas that Jesus presented to his followers, developing theological arguments about predestination and free will or the Trinity, two subjects Jesus was notably silent on, I should note. The rest of the time we're mainly reminding one another of the truths we already know, those that make up the truly important parts of faith.

This section of the gospel of Luke (and Matthew, which is similar) is one of those aspects of Christianity we've heard again and again. Of course, so had Jesus's followers, who were Jewish. The passage from Leviticus makes it quite clear how we should treat those around us: we should give food to those who are hungry; we should respect others, whether through not stealing from them or not lying to them; we should protect those who are unable to defend themselves (the image of a stumbling-block in front of the blind is one that we have mainly forgotten and one we need to revive, as it sums up so well how we place obstacles in the way of those without power in our society); we should not hate, take vengeance, or bear a grudge; in short, we should love our neighbors as we do ourselves.

Jesus's hearers would have known the Torah so well they could have quoted passages like this one to another. They would have been able to discuss this passage at length, drawing on years of rabbinical discussion to lay out all of the nuances that we, as people who are reading it in translation from a distance of thousands of years, cannot hope to see. They would have read it in the synagogues and in their homes; they would have taught it to their children. Knowledge of such passages was not their problem. Jesus isn't telling them to do to others as they would do to themselves because they don't know that Leviticus makes essentially the same statement. He's telling them to do it because they don't.

Such an approach is similar to an old church joke about a new minister. On his first Sunday, he preaches a sermon about how the congregation should love their neighbors as themselves. People compliment his sermon, then go about their lives. On the next Sunday, he preaches the same sermon. People are polite, but clearly confused. He preaches the same sermon on the third Sunday and the fourth Sunday. Finally, people are talking about him to the leadership, so a group of elders goes to talk to him. One of them says, "While we think you're doing a good job, we have a concern about your sermons. We're wondering why you keep preaching the same sermon." The minister replies, "When you start loving your neighbor, then I'll start preaching about something else."

In the same way that the minister's congregation struggles with loving their neighbor, so, too, does the crowd around Jesus. They don't do it because it's almost impossible to do. It goes against everything in human nature. That's the same reason we don't love our neighbors or our enemies, of course. Everything in our beings and in our culture tells us to do the opposite. We have developed over the course of thousands of years to protect ourselves, to survive; our culture tells us that we should look out for number one, that no one else is going to have our interests in mind, so we should. The only person who will try to take care of me is me, so I have to let others take care of themselves. Of course, we see where such a society leads: to unbridled competition, to the strong crushing the weak, to the people in power trampling the marginal, to corporations that care more about profits than people, to churches who focus on budgets and buildings instead of love and justice.

Jesus tells his followers and us to do to others as we would have done to us because we need to hear such a message again and again. This message, in fact, is what separates those who believe from those who don't. Jesus is clear when he reminds us that everyone loves those who love them; returning love we receive is natural. What isn't natural, though, is loving people who hate us, loving people who hurt us, loving people who want to take what we believe to be ours. The gospel doesn't come naturally to us.

I should quickly note that, when Jesus says we are to pray for those who abuse us or we should turn the other cheek, he is writing from a culture that did not discuss spousal or child abuse. He's not talking about that type of behavior. Any Christian should tell a woman or man in a situation of abuse to leave, to get help as soon as possible. We pray for those who abuse others, but we cannot and should not stand idly by while that abuse goes on. If we're going to do to others as we would have done to us, then we work to end such abuse, as no one should endure it. Leviticus (and so many other passages) makes it clear that we protect those who are unable to protect themselves, and abuse victims often have no power; thus, we must help in any way we can.

What Jesus does mean here is that we should not turn our hearts to hate; we should not return violence with violence. Instead, we should love even our enemies, whether they are the ones our country is at war with or the ones down the hall or the ones across the street. If we allow ourselves to turn our neighbors into objects, to cease to see them as people, then we have closed off our hearts to love, so we are unable to receive any. If, however, we find ways to love those whom society would say does not deserve it, we open ourselves up to receive love from one another and from God.

Our minister often quotes another minister who says, "It's just that simple, and it's just that hard." Jesus doesn't remind us of these truths because we've forgotten them; he reminds us because he knows that, while the words are easy to say, they are almost impossible to act upon. We can only do so because God loves us, even though we have done and can do nothing to earn that love. We, then, love others who have done nothing to earn ours. We'll hear this message again and again, and, perhaps, on our best days, we'll act on it. We'll forgive, we'll cease judging, and we'll love, and we'll know what the kingdom feels like.

Questions for Reflection or Discussion:

Who are some people or groups we have trouble loving today?

How can the church help people act out this difficult message of radical love and other such challenging teachings?

True Transfiguration

Transfiguration of Our Lord

Matthew 17:1–9 (also Mark 9:2–9 and Luke 9:28–36)
Exodus 24:8–18

M OST PEOPLE READ THE story of the transfiguration as yet another confirmation of Jesus's divine status, much the way they read the miracle stories. The gospel writers connect this event to Jesus's baptism through the voice from above ("This is my Son, the Beloved" in Matthew), as if the three disciples who are there need another declaration of who Jesus is. With the appearance of Moses and Elijah (but especially Moses), the story lends itself to a metaphorical reading of Jesus as the second Moses (which the lectionary readings reinforce), the one who will lead Israel (and all of humanity) out of slavery and into the Promised Land.

This story, though, seems out of place here. Why is it dropped into the three Synoptic gospels this late into Jesus's ministry? The baptism scene makes perfect sense, coming as it does at the beginning of Jesus's mission. He (or the people around him) need a declaration of his role as the Son of God. Here, though, we're more than halfway through Matthew and Mark and approaching the halfway point in Luke. We've already had the baptism story, and we've seen enough of Jesus by now to either believe or not believe that declaration from the opening chapters of the gospels.

Perhaps this reclaiming of Jesus as Son of God comes here because Jesus has just asked the disciples who they say he is, leading Peter to proclaim him as the Messiah, but then immediately question how Jesus will act as that Messiah when Jesus talks about his own death. Perhaps Jesus or the gospel writers believe that God needs to reassert Jesus's claim, given that Jesus has started talking about his death on a much more regular basis. If the disciples are misunderstanding what it means for Jesus to be the Messiah, God needs to clear this confusion up now rather than as they're going into Jerusalem.

We can also note, though, that the same teaching happens in all three gospels just before this event. Jesus had been talking about what it means to be his disciple, much in the same way he's beginning to talk about what it means for him to be the Messiah. He has told them that they must take up their cross and follow him, that they must lose their lives in order to save them. In the same way that Jesus needs to clarify what his kingdom means, he also, then, needs to make clear what it means to be a citizen of that kingdom. He wants the disciples to understand that they will not be fellow rulers of any sort, that he is not leading a political revolution, but a spiritual one. Instead of being on any type of throne, they will be on a cross, they will be outcasts, and they will be giving up their lives (literally, for almost all of the disciples).

Throughout this passage, we focus on the fact that Jesus is the one who is being changed, though that change is brief and doesn't seem to serve much of a purpose other than declaring who he is yet again. It is actually the disciples (and we) who need to be transfigured. We need a clear vision of Jesus in order to have a true vision of who we are and who we need to be. We, too, are the beloved of God, children of the divine, but that means that we need to change the way we see ourselves and the way we interact with society. Because we all are the beloved of God, we need to move away from society's focus on the self and serve God's other beloved.

Society tells us over and over again that we are the most important people on the planet. In 1992, Bill McKibben wrote a book called *The Age of Missing Information*. He performed an experiment where he had all of his friends help him record every show on every channel on America's largest cable network at the time for a twenty-four hour period (it was in Virginia and had almost one hundred channels). He then spent weeks watching those recordings. He compared that twenty-four hour period to a twenty-four hour period he spent on a mountain, alone. He said that the overwhelming message he received from being on the mountain was that he was small, that he was insignificant in the grand plan of the universe. When he looked for the message from television, though, he wrote, "Everything on television tells you the opposite—that you're the most important person, and that people are all that matter." Society tells us that we are important to ourselves; Jesus, though, tells us we are important to him, which means that we must serve others. We must put our lives aside—lose them, in a sense—and find ways to put others' lives ahead of ours.

However, like Peter's misinterpretation of this event (which I've never understood, for the record; why is it so bad that he wants to build shelters for them?), we have misread the idea of dying to ourselves, or losing our lives. The church has misused this idea of denying the self and others like it to encourage women and minorities (especially) to put others—almost always white males in leadership—ahead of them. Those leaders have used self-denial to reinforce the power structures inside and outside the church, keeping others from speaking truth about injustice.

We need, instead, to listen to the voice affirming Jesus when it tells us to "listen to him." We need to hear what Jesus says throughout his ministry about what true love and self-denial looks like. We must die to our selves, lose our lives, not so that we may serve the powers already in place in the world, but that we might love our neighbors and our enemies, those who look like us and those who don't, that we might bind the wounds of the brokenhearted and lift up the downtrodden. That's true transfiguration.

Questions for Reflection or Discussion:

Where do we see places in society or the church where we're told to focus on ourselves?

How has the church used self-denial as a means of control, and how can the church change that approach?

Spiritual Practices

Ash Wednesday

Matthew 6:1–6, 16–21
Joel 2:12–19

O NE WOULD EXPECT THAT the reading for Ash Wednesday would come from Genesis to talk about humanity's creation from the dust. Job would also work, as well, as he spends much of that book in sackcloth and ashes, and there are numerous reminders of our mortality, as his friends encourage him to curse God and die. While Ash Wednesday is not quite encouraging that behavior, it is the day where we remember our mortality, that we will return to the dust from which we came. It seems the creators of the lectionary calendar missed some obvious opportunities here.

Perhaps the reason they didn't choose the more obvious passages is because we don't really need reminding about our mortality. If we pay attention to the world and our communities at all, we hear enough about the fragility of life. Whether it's the wars going on around the world or the person in the row behind us at church struggling with cancer or our friend whom the doctors just can't determine a diagnosis for, we have too many reminders of the fact that we are not long for this world.

Instead, the passage from Matthew is about how to behave when performing a range of spiritual disciplines, whether that's charity, prayer, or fasting. While the section on fasting seems directly related to Lent, the others seem rather generic, as if they could show up on any Sunday throughout the year. Using them for an Ash Wednesday service seems rather arbitrary, unlike the verses from Joel that sound more like what we would expect.

What the different sections of Matthew have in common, though, is that they are all about focusing on appearances, about the motivation behind what we do, and that seems particularly apt for the season of Lent and Ash Wednesday itself. While many in the progressive traditions take on some sort of Lenten practice, we don't do so with all that much seriousness, if we're honest. We give up chocolate or caffeine, sometimes meat, but we usually are not able to articulate why we're giving those things up in any sort of spiritual way. We tend to think of Lent as a way to get in better physical health, but, spiritually, we struggle to understand what the omission of such products has to do with a stronger faith.

The church used to use Lent as a time of penance, a sort of restitution for the sinful nature of humanity, which was more clearly tied with our mortality. We gave up meat, which was once a luxury, as a way of expressing our recognition that we had sinned. At times, we talked about how we were participating in the suffering of Jesus, as if giving up meat (not to mention chocolate) has any connection to the physical and mental sufferings of Jesus during the last week of his life. We've even used the rationale that we could use the time we once used to make such meals to turn our attention toward God, perhaps even think of God every time we craved whatever it was we had given up. Now, we're not exactly sure what giving such products up means.

There has been a move in recent years to add a spiritual practice during the time of Lent, as if that will help us better understand the spiritual aspect of this season. If we pray more often or write notes of gratitude or read a Lenten devotional, we will see the direct connection between this time of preparation for Easter and our spiritual health. On the surface, that approach does make more sense to us, but we're still not exactly sure why we would do so now, as opposed to Advent to prepare for Christmas. At least giving something up, no matter how small, felt like suffering, and we know that Jesus suffered before Easter.

All of this confusion brings us back to the passage from Matthew and what it might have to say about Lent and our mortality and Ash Wednesday. Jesus is clearly criticizing the religious leaders for their showy practices, ranging from public giving to show how generous they are to their lengthy public prayers to reveal their close connection with God to their overly dramatic times of fasting, where they would heighten the effects of their going without food to illustrate their piety. He ends each of those short sections by reminding them that God rewards what is done on secret, not what we do to convince others of who and how we might be.

In the same way, Ash Wednesday's emphasis on our mortality should ask us to consider why we live our lives the way we do, what our true motivations are. Given that we do have a limited time on Earth, we should be mindful of that time and act out of honest intentions, not from a desire to impress other people. We do not find our treasure, then, by gathering up others' good impressions of us, but by doing what is right and just, where our reward is not worldly acclaim, but a true righteousness that comes from being in line with God's view of justice.

While Jesus is talking about performing actions for appearance's sake, he is not suggesting we keep quiet about people or organizations that need our help. While we should give to those who work for justice, pray for those whom society has pushed to the margins, and give up some of what we desire in order to help those who have less, we should also be vocal about those injustices in the world. We're not drawing attention to our actions, but to those who need help, those whom others have forgotten. We simply have to keep our intentions clear, to make sure that we are doing such work not so that others see our work against injustice, but that they, too, are moved to eliminate suffering and oppression.

We should allow our personal shortcomings, our personal sins, to drive our work to make the world a more just place. If we shift the focus away from ourselves in the public arena and help others see those who suffer, we can more easily admit our own failures. Since we are not the center of attention, we can point toward justice not toward self-righteousness. We can work on those areas where we don't live out the gospel while calling an unjust society into repentance for theirs, as well. If people see God's view of justice rather than our attention-getting actions, we can all be motivated to live more just lives.

Questions for Reflection or Discussion:

Think about what, if anything, you've given up for Lent. Why or how did you choose that and what effect, if any, did doing so have on your life?

What are some practices we could take up or give up during Lent that lead to a more just world?

The Real Problem of Evil

First Sunday in Lent

Luke 4:1–13 (also Matthew 4:1–11 and Mark 1:9–15)
Genesis 3:1–21

BOTH OF THESE STORIES—THE fall of humanity and Jesus's temptation in the wilderness—are familiar to us, and we have trouble believing either of them. Many of us don't believe in a serpent that slithers through the garden to find Adam and Eve and mislead them, and we have real problems with the idea that such a story explains the evil we see around us in the world. Similarly, we struggle with the fact that Jesus could go without food (and especially water) for forty days in the wilderness in the same way that we question the existence of a devil that tempted him—and tempts us—to do wrong.

At our most extreme, we argue as one of my students did about the creation account when he said that it's *just* a story. He meant to dismiss it completely. At our best, we remember that stories, even if we don't believe they're factual, still have truth in them, and so we look for the truth we can find in these stories.

When we look at the Genesis passage, we talk about how it illustrates humanity's tendency to rebel against any kind of restriction or how, for whatever reason, we are always bent on moving away from God instead of toward the divine. We look at Adam's blaming Eve and Eve's blaming the serpent, and we can easily see ourselves, always pointing the finger at other people when we do something that harms us or another. Instead of taking responsibility for our actions and seeking reconciliation, we further divide the community we are in. We might even see an explanation for why we suffer in the world when we read God's curse to Adam and Eve or at least be able to recognize our ancestors' attempts to explain all they had to endure to survive in a world that was not hospitable to them.

In the same way, we read the story of Jesus's temptation as a representation of all of our temptations. Though we might not fast very often, if at all, we live in a culture that daily tells us all we lack. Most of us have the bread we need, so we want artisanal bread and perhaps some expensive cheese and wine to go with it when we know that those things, as enjoyable as they are, do not provide the deep meaning that sustains life. We might not be tempted to rule the world—though most of us have imagined what we would do if we were President or even simply in charge of wherever it is we work—but we have sought after power, even if that was simply within our households or churches or individual relationships. We know what it is like to be tempted with greed and power, so we see ourselves in this account, as well.

In each passage, though, by removing the serpent and the devil, we also remove the idea of an active evil in the world. Many of us would, in fact, argue that there is no active evil, that it is simply a construct of a pre-scientific world that needed an explanation for why bad things occurred. Evil is nothing more than the absence of good, for many of us. If there is evil in the world, it comes from poor choices that people make. Most of the time, that shows up in one individual's hurting another; at its worst, it leads to genocide or racism or sexism or other types of prejudice.

However, if we remove the idea of active evil, we reduce all of the pain and suffering in the world to the level of the individual. Even global actions, such as war, are nothing more than the actions of one person or a small group of people, though those actions have immense consequences for millions of people. This approach leads us to believe that we simply need to change people's hearts (and minds, perhaps), which would lead to a paradise where such events no longer occur. We even remind ourselves that Jesus didn't attack the Roman government, instead focusing on individuals, changing the world one small group at a time.

If we think of evil in this way, though, we ignore the systemic evils that govern our world and shape us in ways we are often not even aware of. We forget that we Americans live in a country driven by an economic system that not only encourages greed, but rewards it, as well. If we want to succeed, we believe we must play by its rules. We want the stock market to increase because our retirement plans are connected to it, and we forget to consider the real people whose lives are affected by the decisions companies make in order for their stock to increase. Companies lay off thousands of employees, and all we see is that we might be able to retire six months earlier.

One of the best examples I've seen of systemic problems comes from housing and race. Researchers asked people how many people, similar to them as far as ethnicity was concerned, they needed to live around them in order to feel comfortable. They had to choose a number from zero to four (one across the street, one behind, one on each side). Most people chose two, a number that many of us would consider a perfectly reasonable answer. These people were perfectly comfortable, they thought, living in a neighborhood where half of the people did not look like them. They ran computer simulations to see what we happen, and, in test after test, the neighborhoods ended up almost completely segregated, much as they are now. We would not consider the individual people racist, but they would end up living in segregated neighborhoods, leading to a city where people of different races seldom interact.

God does not merely call us to resist our personal temptations; these stories remind us that there are evils in the world that go beyond the individual. Even if we were able to remove such desires from our hearts and the hearts of everyone in the world, there would still be systems of oppression. We must work to avoid the temptations we all encounter, but we must also aim to remove the systems that enact evil on such a scale that none of us can avoid it. Only then will the devil depart from us.

Questions for Reflection or Discussion:

Where do we see systemic evil in our world, country, and city?

If there is evil within systems, how do we work for change at that level? And how do we keep from becoming cynical about such change?

The State of the World

Second Sunday in Lent

John 3:1–17
Jeremiah 8:3–15

WE ALL HAVE FELT like the passage in Jeremiah. It's especially easy when I'm writing in an election year. No matter what side of the political divide we fall on, it's easy to believe that the world is headed in the wrong direction. God instructs Jeremiah to tell Israel that they have turned away from God, using one metaphor after another, even going so far as to point out that they don't even have any shame about what they do, as if that makes what they are doing even worse.

We look around America and see continued struggles with racism, sexism, ageism, ableism, and a variety of other prejudices and discriminatory behavior. We talk about micro-aggressions, police shootings, and a glass ceiling that continues to stay firmly in place. The gap between the rich and the poor doesn't simply stay in place, it continues to widen, as the middle class has become something we are nostalgic for. We want the government to step in and find a way to balance out this income inequality at the same time that we don't trust the government to do so fairly. We hear more and more people talking about keeping people out of our country rather than welcoming in the tired and the poor and the huddled masses, forgetting that so many of our ancestors came here willingly or were brought here in literal or economic slavery. Rather than a *United* States of America, we see a country that is more divided than ever.

We especially look at those who disagree with us and think, like Jeremiah, that "they do not speak honestly" and these "people do not know the ordinance of the Lord." I often felt this way when I was in high school, oddly enough driven by my belief that secular things (the things of the world) were corrupting our world. I listened only to Christian music, watched only Christian movies (and it was the 1980s, so they were even worse than the ones produced today), and even stopped watching television for a time. I proclaimed such beliefs loudly, and, though I insisted otherwise, believed that people who did engage with the secular world were not as strong in their faith as I was.

Growing up in the Bible belt, such beliefs were not as uncommon as one might imagine, so I actually had a solid core of friends who, while they didn't quite agree with me in all such beliefs, at least encouraged me down this path. One person, though, recognized that there was a problem with my approach. In my yearbook for my junior year (his senior), he wrote, "May the love of Jesus overcome your hatred of rock n' roll." I wasn't mature enough to recognize his insight then, but I now see that he understood exactly what was driving me.

I wish I could say that I improved as an adult, especially as I moved from a more fundamentalist way of viewing the world to a more progressive one, but I actually just shifted my belief in what it was that was taking the world down the path of evil. In the first sermon I preached as an adult, I railed against businesses such as Wal-Mart, whom I believed were ruining our communities and our economies, choosing part of Jesus's sermon on the mount about not storing up treasures here on earth for my text. I was disappointed when I heard someone leaving the church tell her family that she needed to go by Wal-Mart on her way home.

People often use the passage from John the same way as I used the one from Matthew. If you grew up anywhere near the church, you learned John 3:16, or perhaps you simply saw it on a sign at a sporting event. If you were active in the church, you learned it by heart (probably in the King James version), and you could and did quote it on a regular basis. You probably learned that it is the cornerstone for the Christian faith. Unfortunately, we tended to focus on the parts of it that I would now argue are the less important ones. While we would focus on the fact that "God so loved the world," we usually emphasized the words "believes in him." We turned a verse about God's love into a litmus test.

Our tendency as humans is to try to categorize the world into *us* and *them*, so we need methods of doing so. When I was a teenager, I was an *us*, and everyone who interacted with the secular world was a *them*; even if they were Christians, they weren't the right kind of Christians. As a young adult, anyone who supported big businesses was a *them*, and I was a *us* living in a pure world of my own creation. Not surprisingly, one of my friends told me that I only had one sermon, called "Woe to you, ye generation of vipers." I was Jeremiah reincarnated, it seemed. We all are, though, if we're honest. There's always a group out there who is ruining the world, and we are the ones who must protect it from them.

Of course, we should hold fast to our beliefs, and we should work to make the world a better place. We should seek to bring God's kingdom to earth, to have God's will be done, on earth, as it is in heaven. In doing so, though, we must not vilify those who disagree with us. As Anne Lamott writes, "You can safely assume you've created God in your own image when it turns out that God hates all the same people you do." God calls us not to alienate those we disagree with, but to understand them, to love them, even while we speak out against those beliefs and actions that go against God's vision for the world. Jesus spoke honestly about individuals' and society's failures to live up to God's love, all while living out the love, and he calls us to do the same.

Though we often make children memorize John 3:16, we completely forget about the verse following it: "Indeed, God did not send the Son into the world to condemn the world, but in order that the world might be saved through him." We spend too much of our time condemning the world, forgetting that God, through Jesus, showed us that we should spend our time loving it. That is the way we bring God's kingdom to earth, not through force or argument, but through the unconditional love of Jesus.

Questions for Reflection or Discussion:

What are some issues or ideas we use to divide people into *us* and *them*?

Where are places we or others condemn people or the world when we should be finding ways to love people?

Turning Over the Tables
Third Sunday in Lent

John 2:13–22

UNLIKE THE OTHER GOSPELS, the author of John puts Jesus's turning over the tables in the temple at the beginning of his ministry. We've just had Jesus's first miracle, performed even before it was "his time," as he said, and now here the supposed Messiah is wrecking the temple. Like the other accounts, Jesus is upset by the commerce taking place where there should be worship. When people went to the temple, they needed to have the right sacrifice—the cattle, sheep, and doves mentioned—and it was quite difficult to transport those animals the long distances that people would travel to Jerusalem.

The fact that Roman coins had images of Caesar on them exacerbated the problem. Thus, Jews would have to exchange their money to get temple money—explaining the money changers—to buy the sacrifices they needed to meet their religious obligations. None of this setup would be a problem, save for the fact that everyone involved used this plan to make money from people who often could not afford it. The exchange rate was never in the people's favor, but always benefited those who offered what they would call a service. Everything was done in the name of keeping the religion pure, making the problem even worse.

We often feel as frustrated with the economic and religious problems in our society, as we see rampant inequality, as a vast array of companies take advantage of those who can least afford it. We see Check into Cash businesses in the poorest neighborhoods where there are also no grocery stores, only convenience stores where people pay two or three times what they should for what little food such places offer. Rent-to-own businesses require people to pay four to five times the amount of what appliances should cost because people in poverty cannot afford to pay one lump sum for such purchases, having to eke out monthly payments for years. Such an approach locks people into low quality housing, as well, as they cannot afford to save for a down payment, just making ends meet from month to month.

Unlike Jesus, though, we don't know where to go to turn the tables over, to drive people out with a whip of cords. We feel frustrated and impotent because we don't know how to effect change. We might want to go in to one of these businesses and toss over their washers and dryers or tip over shelves of cans and boxes of processed foods, but we wonder what good even that would do. The business would receive the insurance money and be up and running within a matter of days, and there are other such businesses around every corner. We would be arrested, charged with destruction of property. Some people might even consider us a terrorist, as we would be calling capitalism into question. We don't know what to do when we are stuck in a system that perpetuates such inequalities day after day.

We feel like a group of men in a short story by Stephen Crane called "The Open Boat." Four men—a cook, correspondent, oiler, and captain—are in a lifeboat after a shipwreck, and they are trying to get to shore. The waves keep coming, though, and they feel as if nature is indifferent to their plight, a mark of Naturalism, a literary movement near the end of the 19th century through the beginning of the 20th. The narrator writes, "When it occurs to man that nature does not regard him as important, and that she feels she would not maim the universe by disposing of him, he at first wishes to throw bricks at the temple, and he hates deeply the fact that there are no bricks and no temples." They cannot do anything about nature, so they must endure it.

We also believe we cannot do anything to solve the problems of a system that perpetuates such problems. We perform small works: give to a food bank, serve the homeless a meal, help build a house for low-income residents, send money or food to victims of natural disasters, house the homeless in our church for a week two or three times a year. We don't know—and sometimes don't believe—that such actions do any good at all. It's easy to feel helpless in the face of such problems, problems that seem so much larger than we are.

As he so often does, though, Jesus wants to draw attention to what is truly important in religion, though he does so this time much more dramatically. He wants people to see that it isn't sacrifice that God requires, and it's certainly not meeting a list of requirements; instead, it is a heart of devotion and worship that God wants in the temple. God isn't concerned with our following a list of rules; God is concerned about our loving God and neighbor. In fact, Jesus knows that these people will be back there the next day, having set up again to cheat the people out of their money, all in the name of religion.

However, that doesn't stop him from spending the next few years of his life healing individual people, feeding people who are hungry, treating women and outcasts as equals, loving everyone he meets. He reminds us that the dramatic actions are not what we do every day to change the world, to bring the kingdom. Richard Selzer, a doctor who writes creative nonfiction, tells the story of a doctor he learned from in medical school. That doctor, Hugh Franciscus, performed a cleft palate reconstruction on a girl who was already dead in the dark of night all to make her mother happy. Selzer reflects at the end of his essay: "I would like to have told him what I now know, that his unrealistic act was one of goodness, one of those small, persevering acts done, perhaps, to ward off madness. Like lighting a lamp, boiling water for tea, washing a shirt."

Most of us cannot change the system by throwing it over, literally or metaphorically. We can, though, perform these small, persevering acts for everyone we meet. We can love them as Jesus loved, believing that enough such actions will bring the kingdom while everyone is looking for the dramatic action that our world so values.

Questions for Reflection or Discussion:

What are actions we can take to try to reduce the inequalities in our economic system?

What have other people done for you, even if small actions, to help you during difficult times?

Why Evil Exists

Third Sunday in Lent

Luke 13:1–9
Exodus 20:1–17

ONE OF THE QUESTIONS that almost everyone who has ever encountered Christianity or religion of any kind has asked is about the nature of evil. There are books written about why bad things happen to good people. There's an entire branch of philosophy, theodicy, trying to explain how a god that is all good and all powerful allows evil to exist in the world. People have been struggling to find an answer to this question for centuries, and they have failed for just as long.

Essentially, we come up with one of two approaches, both of which have their limitations. The first is that God allows evil to occur because there is some larger plan in place that we, as humans, cannot see. Thus, when something awful occurs in our lives, we are encouraged to remember that God is ultimately in control and that, overall, the good will prevail. Not only is such an answer small comfort for someone who has just watched their child die after suffering for months, if not years, it implies that God doesn't care about such suffering. If God is all powerful and all good, then God should have been able to design a universe or plan where such suffering is not necessary for that greater good.

There's a sub-argument to that one that blames Satan for such evil in the world. Some people would assert that God created the world as good and perfect, but Satan has corrupted it, which is what leads to such suffering. Again, though, if God is all powerful, then there is no good answer as to why God ever allowed (or continues to allow) Satan to have any influence. That question pushes us right back to the idea of the ultimate plan.

Humanity also gets the blame if we read the story of Genesis literally. God created a perfect world, the argument goes, but we humans rebelled against God, which led to the corruption of the good in the world. If we ask why God allowed that to happen (assuming God is also all-knowing, which usually goes with all-powerful), we come back to the overall idea yet again.

The other option, then, is to lessen the power of God. That argument states that God is not all powerful, simply more powerful than humanity (the comparison is often made with an ant and a human, with humanity as the ants and God as the human). Thus, when awful events occur, God is with us in our suffering, but there was nothing God could do to prevent that event from happening. God is innocent of any involvement with the evil, but God is also not the power that many of us thought when we were younger.

With such thoughts in mind, we can now see what Jesus has to say about the subject. In the passage from Luke, some people (we're not told who) tell him about Pilate's killing some Galileans, seemingly because they were making a sacrifice to God. We don't get any context for this comment, nor do we know what people were seeking from Jesus. We might assume that they were sharing news they thought he might want to hear about how Rome was oppressing Jews, yet again, but we can't even be sure about that.

Jesus, though, takes this opportunity to try to dispel a prevalent myth of the day. He asks the people who brought the news (and anyone else who was around) if those who died did so because they were worse sinners. After he states that they were not, he gives them another example, that of a tower that collapsed, killing eighteen people. He asks the same question about their sinfulness, then points out that they were also not worse sinners. It might seem odd that Jesus would add this additional example, but he wants to broaden the idea of suffering. In the news the people bring him, a person—Pilate, in this case—is responsible for the evil. Thus, it's easy to argue that the evil simply came from someone who is evil. In the second example, though, a tower falls, so no person is to blame. If that's the case, then, the implied question is whether or not God had anything to do with it.

Jesus wants to be clear that God does not punish people in these physical ways for their sins, a belief common at the time. Whether the problem is personal evil or natural disasters, God does not play chess with the universe, moving one piece because it is sinful and another because it is not. However, Jesus also doesn't give any answer to the problem of evil in the world. He doesn't go on to explain why such events do occur; he simply explains away one reason why they do.

In fact, instead of answering the question, he essentially tells his listeners that the question isn't even worth asking. He tells them that they should repent or they will perish as the Galileans and the people killed by the tower did. He can't mean that last part literally, as he's just made it clear that our sinfulness has no connection to whether or not we will die in such an act; thus, he must mean it metaphorically (or spiritually). Essentially, he's telling his listeners (and us) that we shouldn't be focused on answering the age-old question of where evil comes from, but that we should live a life that avoids evil.

Jesus treats evil as something that simply is; it exists in the universe, and we must deal with it, even if we don't know why it exists. That brings us to the ten commandments (the Exodus version; the one in Leviticus is slightly different). Rather than a set of rules we should or shouldn't post on government buildings, this passage is a guide to the way we should live to avoid perpetuating evil in the world. The first four verses tell us we should love God, while the last six tell us we should love others.

The best way to deal with the question of evil in the world is to connect to those around us, to gather together in community. If we steal or envy or commit adultery, we will ruin that community, which is why God provided the Israelites with these particular rules. As Jesus wants the people to repent, God wants people to treat each other humanely, not to dehumanize others. When Pilate kills Galileans, he is taking away their humanity (literally), so the people must gather around their families and comfort them. When the tower falls, the people must provide support to those friends and families of the dead. Evil will continue to exist, and we will always wonder why. The only thing for us to do, then, is to love those we come into contact with and live as humanely as possible.

Questions for Reflection or Discussion:

What types of evil or suffering in the world today leads people to question God's role in those events?

What can we do for people who are suffering to try to help them through such difficult times?

Reconciliation

Fourth Sunday in Lent

> Luke 15:1–3, 11–32
> II Corinthians 5:16–21

T HE PRODIGAL SON (AS many people call it) is one of Jesus's most well-known parables, and we read it in a wide variety of ways. Some of us use it to talk about the son who goes away from home (we've even come to think the word *prodigal* means something about disobedience or rebellion when it actually refers to his ways of spending) and the grace his father shows when he returns. Some people also identify with the older son, the one who does everything right, but who does not receive the fatted calf for a party with his friends. We believe we should get more credit than we do, much like this older son.

The parable, though, really isn't about either one of the sons, despite the name we have given it, which is not actually in the Bible. The parable is about the father, despite his showing up less frequently than the two sons. When we look at the entire fifteenth chapter of Luke, we see three parables that all involve something or someone that is lost, but the focus is not on what/who is lost, but on the joy that is involved on finding it/him. Jesus's goal in these parables is to show the Pharisees and scribes the breadth of God's grace and how it reaches beyond their standard, religious view of who is in the kingdom and who is not.

However, this parable ends differently than the other two. In the parable of the lost sheep, the shepherd finds his sheep and wants his friends to rejoice with him, while in the parable of the lost coin, the woman finds the coin and says what the shepherd says, almost word for word. In the final parable of the chapter—a much longer parable, four times as long as the previous two combined—the son comes home, and we actually see the rejoicing, but the parable doesn't end with the rejoicing. Instead, it ends with the father's speech, and we never see the older brother's reaction. We don't know if the older brother sees the father's argument and goes in to the party or returns to the field or somewhere else, unconvinced and still upset by his father's actions.

The passage in Second Corinthians explains that Jesus is God's attempt to reconcile us to God, despite the ways in which we try to separate ourselves. Traditionally, people have read Jesus's death on the cross as an atonement for our sins, that we needed Jesus to take our place in death, so we could go to heaven after we die. People certainly interpret this passage that way, but it's not the only way to read it. Instead, we can also see that God sent Jesus here as an ambassador for God (to use Paul's language), that he was someone who speaks on behalf of God to remind us how we should live to reconcile not only with God, but with one another.

Jesus reconciled the world to God through his interactions with people, the way he met everyone he encountered with unconditional love, the way he treated the outcast and the minority and the enemy, whether Roman or Samaritan. He lived a life of reconciliation, attempting to bring people not only to God, but one another, whether they were tax collectors or prostitutes or Pharisees or scribes. Then, Jesus entrusted the ministry of reconciliation to us.

Most of us would say we want reconciliation. We celebrate when formerly warring sides come together and declare peace, as in Ireland in the 1990s. We mourn when groups continue to kill one another and destroy wide swaths of land, such as in Israel and Palestine. Even in our interpersonal relationships, we seek reconciliation. We try to heal old family struggles and bring back the alienated child or parent. We hope co-workers will see our intentions in what we suggested in a meeting, that we were not attacking them personally. We know the world is a better place when reconciliation occurs, when we come together in various communities, when we see our commonalities more than our differences.

Unfortunately, reconciliation is difficult, much more difficult than we will often admit. We must be willing to confess our failings, where we were wrong. We must be willing to compromise, to give in and let others have their ways when we want ours. We must be willing to remove our egos, to let go of our desires and wishes. We must even be willing to let go of what we know to be right, to let someone we still believe is wrong to carry the day. Most of us would say we want reconciliation, but we are seldom willing to do the work to make it happen.

The father in Jesus's parable does not ask his youngest son how much money he has spent; he does not give him a lecture on sound money management. The father is right, and the younger son is wrong, but the father doesn't care. The father is simply overjoyed that his youngest son has come home alive and that he will continue to live, even if he continues to live in the wrong way. This acceptance is the grace of God in narrative form, a reminder that Jesus wants us to reconcile with God so much that God will overlook all of our many failings instead of reminding us of them.

This parable, though, doesn't end with the older brother understanding this truth, as far as we can tell. Instead, it ends with the lesson we need to hear in the same way the older brother needs to hear it. It doesn't end with reconciliation, just as so many of our interactions in life don't. Jesus is giving us the ministry of reconciliation here, reminding us that the older brothers of this world—sometimes they are us and sometimes they are those around us—need this reminder on a daily basis.

Reconciliation is amazingly difficult, but, as Kassie Temple, a woman who worked with Dorothy Day said, "Just because something's impossible doesn't mean you shouldn't do it." Our job is to reconcile ourselves to God and to others and to work for that reconciliation in the world. We might not have the party with the fatted calf or we might receive it when we come home; either way, we must hear what Jesus is saying here, overlook all of the wrongs we have done and others have done to us, and to look to Jesus as the model of how to love and accept those around us.

Questions for Reflection or Discussion:

What are things that keep us from reconciliation, personally and more broadly, such as nationally or globally?

Where are places we see a need for reconciliation in our lives and world today?

The Walking Dead

Fifth Sunday in Lent

John 11:1–45
Ezekiel 37:1–14

JESUS'S RAISING LAZARUS FROM the dead is probably one of the most challenging passages for people who don't read the Bible literally. Miracles, in general, cause problems, but a miracle on this scale magnifies those problems. There are certainly other stories of Jesus's raising people from the dead—the widow's son and the Centurion's daughter, for example—but those are briefer stories, less dramatic, in some way. In this story, Jesus seems to purposefully delay his visit to Mary and Martha in order to be sure that Lazarus is, in fact, dead. He also willfully raises Lazarus in front of a crowd, unlike other stories where he either sends people out of the room or simply finds himself among people. Here, he asks Mary where they have buried Lazarus and allows everyone to come with them, even though he knows he is about to perform such a miracle.

Then, on top of all of that public display, he has someone else remove the stone. Obviously, if Jesus can raise someone from the dead, he can cause the stone to move, but he has someone else move it out of the way. He prays publicly, even stating that he is doing so for the sake of the crowd. His prayer isn't even for the ability or power to raise Lazarus from the dead. He simply thanks God for having heard him. He doesn't ask God to hear him; he simply assumes God will do so.

Yet another complication is that this story is only found in John, the latest gospel, and the least reliable. The fact that this recounting is in John certainly explains why it is so different from the other stories of resurrection, as the author of John often portrays Jesus quite differently. There are no parables in the gospel of John, and Jesus has a tendency to hold forth at great length. The longest speeches of Jesus are in John, going on for more than one chapter just a bit later in the gospel.

We're much more comfortable with the passage from Ezekiel, which also seems to be a resurrection story, but it is clearly metaphorical. Ezekiel is told to prophesy to a valley of dry bones, and those bones come back to life. It is a vision Ezekiel is recounting, which is meant to illustrate that God has not forsaken Israel, that the country will rise again, in some sense. The idea of opening graves here is not literal, as Jews at this time didn't have the same ideas of afterlife and resurrection that many had in Jesus's time. They simply believed in *sheol*, the grave, which is much more similar to the Greek idea of Hades than to any New Testament idea of heaven.

Some people read this vision from Ezekiel as a prophetic dream about a future state of Israel, a way of God's promising that, no matter how long it took, the Jews would have a homeland again, as they do now. Reading it, though, as a prophesy of a future resurrection, the second coming of Christ, as others do, misses the historical context of how Jews saw the idea of death. It's interesting, then, that it is often paired with the passage from John. We seem to like the metaphor, but the actual resurrection story worries us. If we can pair the metaphor with the allegedly literal, we avoid having to deal with the possibility of a true resurrection.

A literal resurrection bothers us, at least in part, because we've never seen one. All of our experiences and all of the evidence we know of tells us that death, at least on this plane of existence, is final. People die, and they stay dead. We don't pray over dead bodies, hoping or believing that God will raise the people we love from the dead. We mourn their loss, and we grieve, and we even wish that they were still alive, but we don't believe that they will come back from the dead, even if we believe in a literal heaven. Thus, we question the veracity of this story, and we turn it into a metaphor about some life after death or even about the life we should be living here.

I'll admit that I almost always deal with this story the same way. I wonder, though, what it would look like if we took this story literally, if we believed that Jesus had the power to raise the dead. By extension, we don't have to believe that God still raises the dead, but we do have to question our scientific view of the world. We've come to trust science to tell us how the universe operates and how it doesn't. Science—whether through observation or experiment—tells us that the dead stay dead, and we agree with this evaluation.

This faith in science, though, robs us of wonder and awe at the mystery of the universe and of God. It's easy to criticize early Christians (or even many today) who would believe this story on a literal level. We are more educated, and we know better. If we're honest, though, we know very little about how this universe works and perhaps even less about how God operates in it. Life itself is a mystery. Several pounds of matter in our skulls provide us the ability not merely to function in this world, to survive, but to reflect on that existence, to ask questions about this life and death and resurrection, to create meaning from black specks on white pages, as Kurt Vonnegut once said of writing. We don't truly know how any of these things occur, save for some thoughts about neurochemicals and synapses, and we have no idea whether or not consciousness even exists, though we seem to have one.

In some ways, we have become like the dry bones who insist upon facts and evidence, ignoring the breath that is blowing over us every day. We want to remain dry bones because we are afraid to get up and walk again in the wondrous world that is all around us, filled with people we don't understand, actions we cannot comprehend, beauty we can barely stand. The resurrection might be nothing more than a story the author of John created to illustrate that Jesus is the Son of God. All miracle stories might be crafted for the same reason. They also might be true. There are amazing events that occur every day of our lives. We only have to listen to the breath, to align ourselves with God's spirit, to see them and live in them.

Questions for Reflection or Discussion:

What are things in our world today that keep us from seeing the wonder around us?

How do we balance science and faith in a way that honors both of them and the different ways they see the world?

Street Theater

Palm Sunday

Matthew 21:1–17
Mark 11:1–19
Luke 19:29–48
John 12:12–19

T HE THREE SYNOPTIC GOSPEL accounts of what we have come to call
Palm Sunday follow the same rough outline, with some minor excep-
tions, but John's story is much shorter. John's account is also more Messianic, including comments about what the disciples understood after Jesus
was glorified. That author connects the procession to the resurrection of
Lazarus, claiming that the people went to see Jesus specifically because
of this event. In the gospel of Luke, we have Jesus's concern for Jerusalem
clearly laid out, while the gospel of Mark gives us the additional story of
the fig tree that Jesus curses. The author of Matthew makes the mistake of
having Jesus ride in on two animals, as he tries to show how Jesus's entry fit
with the prophecy from Zechariah, but misreads the repetition, leading to
a strange picture of Jesus straddled across a donkey and a colt.

The major event of the procession is largely the same, with the synoptic gospels adding the turning over of the temple tables, which the author of
John puts much earlier in that gospel account. Most people talk about this
story in two ways: first, Jesus is subverting the expectations of the Jews, as
they wanted their Messiah to be a king in the same way that David was a
king; second, the people who are cheering for Jesus on this day will be the
same ones chanting for his death just a few days later.

This second reading doesn't actually show up in any of the texts, as
there's no evidence that these people are the same people who call for

Jesus's death. Jerusalem was a large city, somewhere between forty and fifty thousand, according to most estimates, and there would have been many more thousands there for the Passover celebration. People ignore these ideas because they want to emphasize the narrative of betrayal that runs throughout the Holy Week narrative. The disciples turned their back on Jesus, so the people must have, too.

The first reading makes much more sense and portrays Jesus as a street performer in a protest movement, creating a work of performance art to protest the Jewish religious establishment. Jesus is calling into question one of the most important beliefs of the Jewish leaders in such a public way, attempting to undercut the entire Messianic narrative, on one level. It is not surprising, then, that Jesus would go to the temple, the most sacred site in Judaism at the time, and literally overthrow the money-making aspect of the faith. In all of the synoptic stories, the Jewish leaders become angry, and, in two of them, they want to kill Jesus.

One theme that has run throughout Jesus's ministry is this questioning of what Judaism has become. Jesus has willfully broken Jewish laws, from not washing his hands before meals to not fasting at the proper time to healing on the Sabbath (and in the synagogues). This story continues that theme and helps explain why the Jewish leaders would want to kill Jesus; thus, it provides a continued development of character and motivation for what will come in a few days.

However, Jesus's procession into Jerusalem is doing more than undercutting the Jewish ideas of their Messiah; he is also subverting the Roman celebration of Caesar and war and empire. Throughout the gospels, the authors have noticeably ignored the Roman reaction to Jesus, partly because he has stayed on the outskirts of the country, avoiding cities like Jerusalem, but also because they wanted to put the blame for Jesus's death on the Jews, not the Romans. Here, though, Jesus is able to criticize both the Romans and the Jews in the same action.

The Romans were known for parading war heroes through towns, and their leaders would come in riding on white horses, while their subjects would lay cloaks along their path. Jesus, then, plays the fool, in the Shakespearean sense, in that he takes what others hold sacred and turns it into farce. Rather than a proud horse, Jesus rides in on a donkey. The crowds are probably not people from Jerusalem, as they didn't know who Jesus was, as the passage in Matthew makes clear. Instead, they are Jesus's followers participating in the farce. In fact, the person Jesus sends the disciples to to retrieve the donkey is probably in on the performance, with Jesus's phrase serving as a password.

Like political protestors who reenact the actions of those in power in an effort to subvert them, Jesus takes what the Romans and the Jews both hold as their core beliefs and mocks them. He wants to show the crowds the absurdity of celebrating those who have come back from battle or those who parade their own importance through towns while putting forth the true ideas he believes in, such as humility and the servant life.

The people in Jerusalem would have been familiar both with the Roman parades, having seen them time and time again, and the Jewish idea of the Messiah. They wouldn't have needed the historical explanation modern readers require in order to understand what Jesus is mocking. This attack on the Romans' belief in honor and pride explains why they would have been equally willing to kill Jesus, moving past Pilate's hesitation to grant the Jews what they wanted. Jesus is not simply engaging in a religious debate, he's engaging in a political one, as well. He is questioning the idea of empire by attacking one of the most visible representations of conquest and war.

Jesus has come preaching a gospel of peace and love and mercy, and the Romans represented the opposite of these truths. The celebrated *pax Romana* was a peace that was only brought into being through war and only maintained through brutality. The Romans loved only themselves and showed mercy to no one. Everything their empire stood for was contrary to the message Jesus had come not merely to preach, but to embody. If we miss this procession as political, we miss a swath of Jesus's ministry. Though he never leads an open rebellion against Rome, he clearly questions all they stand for, this procession a form of passive resistance calling into question their values and beliefs.

Jesus merges the religious and political not because they are the same, but because he wants to attack the problems in both. They can both do good and help others in a variety of ways, but, perverted by a focus on greed and the self, they end up harming those whom they should be serving. Jesus reminds us that humility will ultimately win out over war and that greed can be overturned, as can tables, merely by riding into Jerusalem on a donkey.

Questions for Reflection or Discussion:

What are beliefs or practices in our society that we need to call into question?

Are there ways we can question them through this type of performance? If not, what are ways we can subvert or question them?

The Body and the Blood

Maundy Thursday

Luke 22:7–20
Jeremiah 31:31–34

PROTESTANTS DON'T DO A good job of talking about communion. Episcopalians probably do the best, due to their more direct lineage to Catholicism, where the Eucharist is so serious they offer it not just in a weekly worship service, but usually several times throughout the week. Many Protestants, though, are unable to truly articulate why communion is so important. We stumble along about consubstantiation as opposed to transubstantiation, maybe even bringing in terms, such as "sacramental union," "objective reality, silence about technicalities," or "Pneumatic presence." If you don't know what any of these terms are or mean, don't worry about it; most of us, including me, would be hard pressed to define or explain them. Sometimes the internet really is the best resource.

Most of the time, we talk about communion as a symbolic act with the bread symbolizing Jesus's body and the juice or wine symbolizing Jesus's blood. Our wording, though, sometimes shows we're even uncomfortable with that language, as we sometimes say when giving the bread and juice or wine, "This is the bread of life" and "This is the cup of salvation." Even though we offer the traditional words of institution (the lead-in to communion where we talk about Jesus's breaking the bread and pouring out the wine), we don't like the idea that bread and juice/wine have anything to do with Jesus's physical body.

Catholics believe that it's very much the physical body and blood of Christ, as they contend that the bread and wine become that actual physical body and blood, which is why the Eucharist is the centerpiece of their worship. Flannery O'Connor, a Catholic fiction writer, has the best quote about the divide between how Catholics see this sacrament and how Protestants do. In a conversation with a friend (as she recounts in a letter), she says that her friend describes communion as a symbol. O'Connor responds, "Well, if it's a symbol, to hell with it." She adds in the letter, "That was all the defense I was capable of but I realize now that this is all I will ever be able to say about it, outside of a story, except that it is the center of existence for me; all the rest of life is expendable." I don't know of any Protestants, even those who celebrate communion every Sunday, who would argue that it is the center of existence or even of worship.

The question, then, is what we are to do with communion and why it matters to us. Both passages—the one from the gospel of Luke and the one from Jeremiah—talk about the idea of a new covenant. Traditionally, people have interpreted this phrase through the lens of Old Testament sacrifice. The old covenant was based on offering God sacrifices on a regular basis to atone for our sins. Under the new covenant, Jesus is that sacrifice, and that sacrifice gives humanity forgiveness once and for all. There is no need for another sacrifice, as Jesus is the perfect sacrifice.

Though there are minor references to sacrifice, as Jesus does talk about giving his body and pouring out his blood, these two passages talk much more about forgiveness and acceptance without any conditions. In Jeremiah, God says that the people will know God "from the least of them to the greatest" and God will "forgive their iniquity, and remember their sin no more." God lays out no expectations here, and, in fact, the power inherent in the ancient sacrificial system is undercut completely. As in so many other passages in the prophets, God makes no distinction between the least and the greatest. All people will know God, no matter their social status.

This inclusivity is matched by Jesus's use of a meal as a metaphor for his disciples. Throughout Jesus's teaching, he referred to the kingdom of God as a feast where all are invited, where all are welcome. He taught about not seeking the place of honor at such meals, as the least would be lifted up to those places. He told parables about sending people into the streets to invite people in to the feast. The proclamation of Mary early in the gospel of Luke comes to fruition in the final feast Jesus has with his followers, welcoming all and giving all he has for them.

Jesus is offering unconditional love and grace here, holding nothing back as he has done throughout his ministry. He gives us a glimpse of the kingdom, the next time he will eat this meal with us, as he tells his disciples.

The word *covenant*, though, implies an agreement between two parties. It is strange, given that the passage in Jeremiah talks about how all will know God, that there would be any implication of a covenant between God and humanity. If we are looking at these passages through the lens of inclusion, that word should trip us up.

However, God is not laying out a new set of rules, another book of Leviticus or Deuteronomy. Instead, what God is asking is for us to embody the truth of God, that we would write the law on our hearts, essentially, be the body of Christ. As Christ gives his body and his blood for his disciples and for us, we are called to give that same love and grace to others. We are to eat that feast in a metaphorical sense every day of our lives, not simply celebrate a literal reenactment of it certain Sundays.

Jesus is calling us to welcome everyone to the table, no matter their socioeconomic status or their race or gender or sexual orientation or gender identity or ethnicity or background or ability or past or anything else we can think of that we use to separate us from one another. The law that God writes on our hearts is a law of love and grace because God has forgiven our iniquities; so, too, do we forgive what others have done to us.

Communion is the literal reminder of this calling, not a symbol of one meal at one point in time. It is the idea of the feast that runs throughout Jesus's message, the metaphor for the kingdom of God where all are welcome and will always be welcome. If it's only a symbol, O'Connor is right to discount it; if it serves to speak to us—whether weekly or monthly or quarterly—about the unconditional love and grace of God and our participation in sharing that message, then it helps to bring the kingdom into existence, on earth as it is in heaven.

Questions for Reflection or Discussion:

What did people teach you about communion in the past, and how have your thoughts about it changed?

What are things we let divide us where Jesus's idea of radical inclusivity could help us overcome? And how can we celebrate communion in a way that reflects that idea?

The Cross

Good Friday

John 18:1—19:42

F OR MANY YEARS AND in many churches, people have talked about the
crucifixion of Jesus more than any other event in the Bible, including
the resurrection, which often gets relegated to Easter. While some Christians would argue the empty cross is a symbol of resurrection, many Christians seem more fascinated by the suffering of Jesus than the idea of new life
and certainly more than the inclusive nature of Jesus's ministry. The cross is
the symbol of the church, put up on our churches and inside our churches,
worn around necks and wrists, even tattooed on a variety of body parts. We
can see Paul's influence here, no doubt, as he also seemed to talk about the
cross more than any other subject.

People tend to talk about Jesus's crucifixion in only one way, which
influences why we talk about it so much: Jesus died on the cross to save
humanity from their sins. Note that he wasn't incarnated as a man to save
humanity from our sins, save for the fact that he had to become human in
order to die on the cross; he didn't heal and teach and feed and love to save
humanity from our sins; nor did he give humanity hope that we could, in
some way, overcome the grave in order to save humanity from our sins. The
crucifixion does all of the work, so it gets most of the attention.

This reading of the crucifixion makes sense, given that Jesus was Jewish, and the disciples and early Christians almost exclusively came out of
that Jewish culture. Paul was certainly influenced by Greek and Roman
ideas, and the church spread in that direction rather quickly, but the ori-
gins are clearly Jewish. Judaism was a religion centered around sacrifice,
centered around the idea that God demanded that humanity atone for our

sinful nature in this way. Anyone who reads the Old Testament for the first time is struck not only by the amount of blood shed, but the detail with which the authors lay out those sacrifices. Many new Christians try to read the Bible straight through, only to get stuck in Leviticus or Deuteronomy.

However, there are other ways, perhaps more productive ones, of reading what happens to Jesus. The sign that Pilate has hung on the cross and the Jewish leaders' reaction to that sign give us one entry point into how to read Jesus's crucifixion. Jesus has clearly been stirring up trouble in his ministry. He has angered the Jewish leaders throughout his time, especially in the gospel of John, as the author of this narrative has Jesus turning over the tables in the temple early in Jesus's ministry. He has broken Jewish law on a regular basis, often in the synagogues and in front of the religious leaders. In their minds, Jesus is a political problem they need to deal with.

Pilate, however, also had political reasons for wanting to see Jesus crucified. Ancient Israel was on the outskirts of the Roman Empire, and it had a reputation as an unruly area, often given to uprisings and rebellions. Pilate's job was to keep the peace, and he needed to quickly and efficiently deal with anyone who disrupted that peace. Unlike the portrayal of Pilate in the gospels, historically, he was ruthless, often killing people simply to prove a point. He didn't need convincing when it came to killing troublemakers.

That's why he clearly labels Jesus as the King of the Jews, as he wants to send a message to the other Jews that rebellion is futile and that he will deal with it swiftly and harshly. Pilate only thinks in terms of power, which is why he states quite clearly to Jesus that he has the power to release or kill him. Pilate views the world through the lens of politics and power and kingdoms and force, and he kills Jesus as a political terrorist.

Jesus sees the world through a different lens, one where he is willing to die for what he believes in, one where power comes through passive resistance not retaliatory force, which leads to more war and more violence. Unlike Peter in the garden, Jesus does not take up arms against the soldiers who come to arrest him. Unlike other prisoners, Jesus does not offer explanations or excuses for what he has done. Instead, Jesus goes willingly to crucifixion, not because he is seeking to atone for the sins of humanity, but because he believes his teachings and his life can change the world, and dying this type of death will be one more piece of evidence of how to live a life of love in this world.

There is one other complicating factor in this story of the cross. Jesus is from Galilee, as are almost all of the disciples (most scholars believe Judas was from Kerioth, which was in the south of Judea), and they have come into Jerusalem, the largest city and the center of Judaism. Jesus is probably poor, though there is debate about whether or not he was raised in a lower- or middle-class family. He seems to have renounced any wealth, given that he needs people to support his travels, and Joseph quite likely died when he was young (given his absence from the gospels and the fact that Mary and his brothers come to find Jesus, as if they need his help). We have, then, a group of men from the country (as people in Jerusalem would have seen those from Galilee) who are or have become quite poor.

These are the people who lived near the margins of Jewish society. They have no power in the terms that Pilate thinks of it. As with so many people in poverty before and after Jesus, he receives no real trial, shuffled from one person to another at night, then crucified with thieves as common as he was, economically-speaking. The Romans did not design their system to protect the poor, but the powerful; the Jewish religious structure was designed to reward those already in power and those with wealth, not the poor and outsiders who had to negotiate the complex and extortionary rules of temple sacrifice.

There's a clear connection to the contemporary problems with the death penalty in America, as those without the wealth to defend themselves are much more likely to end up condemned to death than those with access to expensive lawyers. Not coincidentally, those people who can afford better legal support are overwhelmingly white. Even beyond the idea of wealth, though, minority defendants are much more likely to receive a death sentence than those who are white. Those on the margins of our society are just as likely to be put to death as are those on the margins of Jewish society, such as Jesus.

While Jesus is the most famous example of crucifixion, he was far from the only one. Instead, in the Romans' opinion, he was simply one more poor outsider who was causing trouble and who needed to be killed as quickly and publicly as possible. To the Jewish leaders, he was one more Messiah who undercut their message that their way was the only way to God. He had no connections, no one in power to help him when he went too far. Jesus was a victim of his poverty (whether chosen or not) and his politics, and he died an ignoble death as so many did. The one difference is that he chose this death for what he believed in, chose to die as one more example to us of how to live: speaking the truth to those in power, passively resisting that power, even when it cost him his life.

Questions for Reflection or Discussion:

What did you learn about the crucifixion if you grew up in the church (or even outside the church)? How did that understanding shape your view of Jesus and his life?

How can we connect Jesus's death to how we talk about capital punishment in our society?

The Empty Tomb

Easter Sunday

Matthew 28:1–10
Mark 16:1–8
Luke 24:1–12

A S WE OFTEN DO with the Christmas story, we talk about the Easter story as if it were only one story. We combine the synoptic gospel accounts, sometimes even including John, into one partially coherent story, ignoring the differences between the stories. We conflate the stories, at least partly for ease, as we do with the Christmas passages; it's simply easier if we have one telling of who went to the tomb, what happened there, and what happened afterwards. We also might combine the accounts because these two events are two of the most difficult to believe, and we want the easiest story possible.

Mark's telling is the one we tend to ignore, as it ends with the women's not going to tell Peter and the disciples about what the young man in white has said to them. Instead, they are seized with "terror and amazement," so they didn't tell anyone what had happened. This story is even more problematic, given that many scholars believe the gospel ended here. Since Mark was written before the other gospels, that doesn't leave much hope in the Easter story.

Even Luke's account of the empty tomb doesn't add much more to Mark's account. Here the women do go and tell the disciples, but they see the women's telling as "an idle tale." Only Peter goes to look and finds the tomb empty, though he simply goes home amazed. There is more hope here, as at least the women go and tell what they have seen and Peter reacts with his own action, though he needs verification rather than simply trusting the women.

It's worth noting here that one similarity in all of the gospel stories is that women (or a woman) are the ones who go to the gravesite, and they (save for in Mark) go and tell the disciples the tomb is empty. Jesus has been quite clear in his ministry in his acceptance of women and his equal treatment of them, so this inclusion is not a surprise. Unfortunately, neither is the fact that the disciples don't believe the women. Granted, their news is surprising, to say the least, but it is telling that the men don't believe the women, even though, according to all of the gospels, Jesus was quite clear that he would rise from the dead.

The early church honored Mary Magdalene (who goes alone in the gospel of John) as the *apostola apostolarum* or the apostle to the apostles. They saw her as the first person to tell the good news that Jesus had risen, making her the first apostle ("one who is sent forth"). The church, though, changed its view of her by the 6th century, as they turned her into the woman who washed Jesus's feet with her tears and hair, a woman whom they believed to be a prostitute. Even now, if you ask Christians about Mary Magdalene, more than half of them will say she was a prostitute, despite their being no evidence—biblical or otherwise—she was one. Thus, the gospel accounts present women as the ones to bring the most important news of the early church, yet the church quickly began to silence their voices and discredit them, not listening to them, essentially, as the disciples didn't.

What all the gospel stories also have in common is that the women who came to the tomb were afraid, yet they were told not to be. In every telling, save for Luke, oddly, the women are told not to be afraid or amazed, but that they should go and tell Jesus's disciples that he waits for them in Galilee. Even in Luke, the words of the two men obviously provide comfort, as they then remember Jesus's words to them, which is what motivates them to go and tell the disciples. Whatever else this story is, it is clearly a story that is designed to provide comfort and hope. The passage from Matthew is the most obvious example of this hopefulness, as Jesus actually makes an appearance in this telling and tells them himself that they should not be afraid.

This idea of providing comfort, combined with the developing changes in the story—from Mark's ending of "terror and amazement" to Matthew's hopefulness (and to John's clear declaration of hope)—cause people to doubt the historicity of the resurrection. Many scholars, such as John Dominic Crossan and Marcus Borg, talk about a distinction between resuscitation and resurrection. They say that Jesus didn't literally rise from the dead, but that, in some way, he continued to live in and among the disciples. Given that there were a number of such stories about gods at the time, their distinction makes sense. The disciples went through a traumatic loss and wanted to believe that Jesus was still with them, so, they argue that, over the years (Mark was written a good thirty years after Jesus's crucifixion), the story developed into yet another tale of a god who died but who came back from the grave. Jesus's story is, in many ways, no different from those stories, which means that Jesus is not much different, if any, from those other gods, whom we now know to be fictions.

I've struggled with this idea for more than a decade, sometimes believing the resurrection never happened, sometimes believing it could have, very seldom believing it did. It is such an unbelievable action, somehow more difficult to believe than the incarnation and Jesus's raising Lazarus from the dead, that we struggle with it. However, there is at least one thing I've always been able to say about it: Something must have happened, as we have disciples who were once afraid, abandoning Jesus when he is arrested, who are willing, not even months after Jesus's crucifixion, to die for their beliefs. I might not know what that something is, but I have to believe something happened.

Also, even if the story develops and becomes more exaggerated, even if Mark's account that ends with the women's not telling anyone, seized with "terror and amazement" is the most reliable, that story still has an empty tomb. It seems an odd story to create from nothing. If one were to craft a tale to convince people of Jesus's resurrection, the author of that story wouldn't have the story end in such a manner. Instead, it would sound much more like Matthew's account. I can only conclude, then, that people at least believed Jesus rose from the dead, and I have to believe they had a reason to do so. Again, something happened in their lives that was significant enough for them to honestly believe Jesus didn't stay in the tomb. That might not be enough hope for most people, but it makes sense to me intellectually and emotionally, and that's enough for me.

Questions for Reflection or Discussion:

What were you taught about the resurrection if you grew up in church (or even if you didn't), and how did that understanding shape your view of Jesus?

What message of hope does the resurrection provide to those of us who live in a more skeptical, scientific age?

Having Faith

Second Sunday of Easter

John 20:19–31
Acts 4:32–35

P ERHAPS I'VE JUST CHANGED the types of churches I attend over the past couple of decades, but it's been a long time since I heard the "doubting Thomas" label applied as I did when I was growing up. That change could be due to a simple lack of biblical knowledge or use of biblical allusions in common conversation, but I'd like to believe that it's because Christians have changed the way we talk about this story.

For many of us who grew up in the church, preachers and church leaders used Thomas as a way to squelch any discussion or disagreement. If anyone asked difficult theological questions, the leadership would simply tell them not to be a doubting Thomas and remind them of the importance of faith. The leaders would tell the questioners that Jesus emphasized faith, believing without seeing or putting hands in his wounds. Such an approach played out in households as well as churches, as parents used this story to discourage questioning teenagers, often with negative results. Many people simply left the church when parents or leaders did not engage with their honest questions.

Thankfully, there are more and more sermons pointing out that Jesus doesn't chastise Thomas for his supposed lack of belief. Ministers and church leaders are now much more willing to remind us that Thomas is not the only disciple who doubted. When Mary and the other women come from the tomb to tell the disciples that Jesus is not there, those disciples also did not originally believe, with John and Peter running to the tomb to see for themselves, the equivalent of having to put one's fingers in Jesus's wounds.

This story, then, is not a story about not having faith in God's ability to raise Jesus from the dead. It's not an illustration of one disciple's lack of belief without his being able to see clear proof. Thomas is not the quintessential doubter in the gospel story, as everyone in the story of the resurrection questions what they see or hear, rightfully so, as what they see or hear is unbelievable; that's the point of it.

Instead, then, this passage might be more about community than about some sort of unquestioning faith. It is not so much that Thomas doesn't believe that God can resurrect Jesus; after all, he's been following Jesus for three years, and he's seen Jesus raise the dead. If Jesus can call Lazarus from the tomb after four days (a story in which Thomas figures rather prominently, as he questions the logic of going to Jerusalem), God can clearly raise Jesus after three days. Rather, the problem here is that Thomas doesn't believe the other disciples, much as the disciples didn't believe the women.

Thomas had been travelling with this group of disciples for three years, from what we can tell. Granted, people would have come and gone during that time, but all of the gospels present a core group of followers who stayed with Jesus throughout his ministry. They ate together, slept together, worshiped together, watched and heard Jesus together. After all of that time and a supposed shared purpose, they should have had enough faith in one another to believe that the others would not mislead one of their own.

While there were conflicts within the group—whether that was people jostling for position at the right hand of God or ostracizing Judas because of where he came from—there should have been some sort of cohesion here. There's no reason for anyone to believe that any of Jesus's main followers would purposefully lie to one of the others, especially around something so important as Jesus's death. It's not as if the disciples were prone to playing cruel practical jokes on each other. Instead of showing a lack of faith in God's abilities, this passage illustrates humanity's lack of faith in each other, even when there is no reason to doubt one another. That type of doubting is what leads churches to falter or split rather than come together under a shared purpose.

In the passage from Acts, that author portrays the church as clearly unified under a shared purpose. The post-resurrection church has now come together as one, putting aside whatever differences there are to truly trust one another. Instead of questioning one another, they now share their possessions in common, making sure that none of them have any physical needs that go unmet. They have ceased to care about their concerns and shifted their efforts to satisfying the needs of others.

In order to do so, they have to trust one another at a level most of us never experience. If they no longer own their land or houses or possessions, they are completely at the mercy of the church. If the apostles in this passage decide to stop distributing the funds from those sales, people will go hungry or have no place to live. The early church knew, though, that no one in their community would do so because they were acting out the teachings of Jesus. They were now bound by an unconditional love as exemplified in Jesus's death and resurrection.

Whenever we encounter this passage, we almost always respond with skepticism. American society is built around the idea of individualism and being able to provide for oneself. The early church shows us another way, one that is centered around radical faith in the Christian community. While we might not be able to recreate such an environment, it should inform the way we think about communities. We should put people in positions of leadership who act on such faith to create places of radical inclusivity and trust, knowing that we all have come to that community out of a shared belief in Jesus's teachings of unconditional love and acceptance. Then, no one will have need to doubt one another, and we will believe what the others have to teach us.

Questions for Reflection or Discussion:

What are issues that divide the church today, that cause us to distrust one another?

What are ways we can create communities that look more like the early church?

Being Human
Third Sunday of Easter

Luke 24:13–35 (also Luke 24:36–49 and John 21:1–14)

T HESE THREE POST-RESURRECTION STORIES about Jesus have one small detail in common: they all involve food. In the Emmaus story, Jesus breaks bread with the two travelers, which enables them to see him for who he is. In the second passage from the gospel of Luke, Jesus specifically asks for something to eat, leading the disciples to give him a piece of broiled fish to eat. In the reading from the gospel of John, Jesus is the one who has prepared some food, as he has fish cooking on a fire, along with some bread, and he encourages the disciples to bring some of the fish they have caught and have breakfast.

One way people often teach or talk about these stories is that they serve as evidence of the resurrection, or they at least once filled that role in the early church. Even if they are not historically true, early Christians told them to show that Jesus physically rose from the dead. The emphasis in the second passage from the gospel of Luke on Jesus's actually eating the fish in their presence is the strongest example of such a use for these stories. If Jesus could eat a piece of fish, then he was clearly not some sort of ghost or spirit come back from the dead; instead, he was in human form once again, even if changed in some way (the story of Thomas's putting his hands in Jesus's wound serves the same purpose).

More recently, people have adapted that interpretation to talk about the importance of Jesus as a physical human being, someone who inhabited a body, in the same way that most of us talk about the incarnation. Jesus's eating food reinforces the idea that he was a human who had human needs. If he needed to eat, then he struggled with hunger, which easily leads us to believe that he struggled with other human limitations, ranging from aches to serious pain. We talk about Jesus as a body, not just as a spirit in the same way that we also are our bodies, as well as our spirits. Such an approach is healthy, as it keeps our theology from becoming too abstract.

This type of thinking runs throughout the gospels, as we see Jesus touching people to heal them when he could, we assume, speak words and achieve the same result. He lays his hand on people's heads or touches their tongue, for example. Similarly, he asks people to perform actions with their bodies, such as going to wash in the river, as if he wants to remind them that they, too, are bodies, with all the limitations that come with them. These stories can certainly serve to drive home this point that Christianity is as much about the body as it is the soul.

That reading works fine, and it's one that we need to hear on a regular basis. However, these stories also serve another purpose, one that we also need to talk about more often. When Jesus is walking on the road to Emmaus with two of his followers, they don't recognize him, a fact that seems either confusing or supernatural. Either the disciples are so distraught with grief that they can't recognize the person they have loved enough to mourn, which doesn't seem plausible, or God prevents them from recognizing him in some way, perhaps to achieve the result at the end of the story.

There is another way of reading this passage, though, one that is more metaphorical in nature. Many scholars question the validity of most, if not all, of the post-resurrection stories, arguing that the early church told them as ways of remembering Jesus, not as factual accounts of what happened after Jesus's death. Jewish readers might or might not have believed these stories to be historically accurate, but they also didn't think about historicity in the same way contemporary readers do. They read stories on multiple levels, always reading on a symbolic or metaphorical level, while also reading on a literal plane. For them, then, the story would mean much more than the fact that two people were walking on a road and had a physical encounter to Jesus.

The important part of this story is that they don't recognize Jesus until they sit down with a stranger and share bread with him. It's easy enough to see this scene as an echo of the last supper and point out that they only recognize Jesus in the act of what we now call communion, but we don't need that echo to understand why this scene matters so much. The only reason they are able to see Jesus is because they insist that he stay with them, that he share a meal and a place to stay with them. Then, when they are at the table, they recognize him. Whether or not the stranger is truly Jesus is beside the point. What is important is that they encountered a stranger on the road, and they engaged him in conversation, then welcomed him into their home and shared a meal with him. They treated him as a human being with human needs, the most basic of needs, in fact: food, shelter, and companionship. After they have shared all of those necessities with him, they see Jesus.

In the same way, we see Jesus whenever we engage in acts of hospitality, when we treat others as the human beings they are. There are obvious examples of feeding those who would not be able to eat otherwise or providing shelter for those without homes, but we can also provide daily hospitality to those who need it. We can take time to talk with that co-worker who seems to do nothing but complain, to try to understand why he is so unhappy about life. We can share a conversation with the older woman on the park bench as we sit outside eating our lunch.

Even beyond those actions, we can speak out in support of those people society portrays as less than human, whether because of their race or gender or sexual orientation or gender identity or ability. We can treat people as humans, not as labels that divide us from one another. We can ask them about their parents or their work or how their day was, and we can truly listen to them, remembering that they have bodies as well as souls. Of course, we can also break bread with everyone we meet, recognizing all of our human needs for shelter, food, and companionship. By doing so, we, too, will see Jesus.

Questions for Reflection or Discussion:

Where are places in our society where we need to show more hospitality?

How could the church minister more to people who have bodies, not just souls?

Abundant Living

Fourth Sunday of Easter

John 10:1–10
I John 3:16–24

THIS PASSAGE FROM JOHN is one of those a particular strand of Christians use to argue that Jesus is the only way to obtain salvation. He is the one and only gate, they argue, and all others are thieves and bandits who only want to steal, kill, and destroy (your soul, they imply or even state). If people would simply accept Jesus as their Lord and Savior, pray the sinners' prayer, then they could have life and have it more abundantly.

It's true that the gospel of John uses figures of speech that lay out that Jesus is the way to salvation (John 14:6 is the most common example, as there the author shows Jesus saying that no one receives salvation, save through Jesus). Most scholars respond to these passages by pointing out that the gospel of John was written much later than the other gospels (some scholars put it as late as 150 CE, at least fifty years later than the gospels of Matthew and Luke, perhaps even closer to seventy years later) and that the structure and theology of this gospel is rather different than the other three.

In this gospel, the parables are largely gone, though Jesus does use metaphors on a regular basis, as in this passage. Instead, we have long passages of Jesus simply holding forth (almost three full chapters in one place) instead of the shorter, dialogue-rich passages in the other three gospels. Theologically, Jesus is much more willing to admit he is the Messiah, the King of the Jews in this gospel, whereas he was more evasive in the other three. It also has the most developed post-resurrection theology, as the early church had more than a hundred years to think through how they thought about that event by the time this gospel was written.

Thus, at least from that point of view, it's clear why this gospel has many more passages that seem to limit who gets in and who doesn't when it comes to some sort of eternal salvation. The Jesus in this gospel seems much clearer on the requirements to attain an eternity lived with him. In this passage, we see that we need only to follow Jesus's voice, and we will have life, and have it more abundantly.

However, even in that reading and interpretation, we seem to be adding a number of ideas from other places. While Jesus does say that all those who came before him are thieves and bandits, we have no idea who he is talking about in this passage. He could be referring to those magicians and political leaders who traveled around Israel on a regular basis, claiming they were the Messiah, those whom Gamaliel references in Acts as having been put to death, only to see their followers scatter. Some contemporary Christians argue that they are religious leaders, such as Gautama Buddha or Confucius. Some, unfortunately, miss the part about the people coming before Jesus, and they reference Muhammad, among others.

Given Jesus's constant critiques of the Jewish religious leaders, it could just as well be them. Some people might read this passage, then, as Jesus's clearly distinguishing Judaism from the Christianity he came to establish (some scholars argue that Jesus never intended to create something new; instead, like Martin Luther, he only wanted to reform the religious tradition he was a part of). Those who listen to the religious leaders will only suffer, while those who follow Jesus will truly live.

This passage also leads some to conclude that Jesus wants us to have financial success, the prosperity gospel, essentially. If we have life abundantly, that means we will have more than enough of everything we need, they argue. We need money to live, so we will have more than enough, the logic goes, so those who truly hear Jesus's voice will have financial rewards, as that helps give us abundant life.

None of these readings line up with everything else we know about Jesus, his teachings, and the early church, though. They seem to impose a reading—Jesus is the only way to salvation, and believing in him will bring rewards we cannot imagine, whether financial or otherwise—on a passage that is about something else altogether. The point of this passage is not how one finds salvation, as Jesus never lays out a road map for how to do so (the sinners' prayer, for example, is nowhere in the Bible).

Rather this passage is about the love Jesus has for humanity, about how desperately he wants others to hear his voice. Rather than viewing the sheep here only as those who have obtained some sort of salvation, the sheep serve as a representation for humanity, in general, as we often follow thieves and bandits who seem intent on harming us in some way. We are so desperate for relationships, we will follow anyone who promises to care for us, no matter what they do to us along the way.

Jesus, however, promises to give us this abundant life, leaving it with no description. The passage from I John, though—probably not written by the same person—shows us what an abundant life looks like: it's one we live for others, not for ourselves. It is a life of action and truth, not meaningless promises and well-intentioned thoughts. It is a life where we see someone in need, and we find a way to help her or him. Jesus lived a life of radical inclusivity and sacrifice, a life where love superseded every other religious teaching of his day, and he calls us to do the same.

An abundant life is one where we love those we encounter, no matter their sexual orientation or ability or gender or race or ethnicity, and we love them enough to set aside our lives, our wants, our demands, to help them attain theirs. We act on Jesus's command and love others in the name of Jesus, and we, then, receive an abundant life, a life so overfull we can barely stand it. When we love others and think of their needs, our lives become more complete, as we see the kingdom of God everywhere we look, and it is so beautiful, we can only feel the fullness of the world.

Questions for Reflection or Discussion:

What are ways we've developed to decide who's "in" and who's not, historically and now?

What does an abundant life look like, according to your church?

New and Improved

Fifth Sunday of Easter

John 13:31–35
I John 4:1–11
Acts 8:1–18

I N THE READING FROM the gospel of John, we see one of those familiar passages where Jesus is telling the disciples to love one another. What's out of the ordinary about this passage is that Jesus says he's giving them a new commandment, first stating simply that they should love one another, then expanding that idea to say they should love one another as he has loved them. Perhaps we've heard this passage too many times—even those who didn't grow up in the church—but nothing about this commandment sounds new.

Part of the problem is that we have heard this idea, in one form or another, many times throughout life. For those of us who grew up in the church, we heard it hundreds and thousands of times. A more significant problem, though, is that we never heard it at all, and we still don't. None of the other gospels have Jesus saying exactly what he says here, though he clearly gets a similar idea across. What most of us hear in this passage is that we should love our neighbor as ourselves, the more popular passage that people throughout America, whether Christian or not, could identify.

Here, Jesus is saying something slightly different, but the difference is important. Rather than simply pointing out that we should love our neighbor as we do ourselves, Jesus wants our love for one another to mirror his love for humanity. While we do love ourselves more than is usually healthy, we also turn against ourselves on a regular basis. We criticize and judge ourselves, often much more harshly than others do. We refuse to forgive ourselves long after others have already done so. At the times we often need it the most, we are unable to love ourselves.

Jesus's commandment, then, is new, as it's an expansion of the traditional command to love our neighbor as ourselves—a verse from the Old Testament that Jesus was reminding his hearers of, rather than presenting it as something they had never heard—to love each other with the unconditional love of Jesus. This passage from the gospel of John is part of what most scholars refer to as Jesus's "farewell address," a long passage where he (or the author of the gospel) is summing up Jesus's ministry. He is reminding them, then, that love is the cornerstone of that ministry.

In fact, it will be the cornerstone of the early church, as Jesus points out that others will know they are Christians by their love. This approach is new to Jewish hearers who have become accustomed to people's knowing them by their outward religious practices or even how they dress or what they eat. Instead, Jesus wants them to continue his ministry by loving every person they meet. A couple of decades ago, I was teaching a book—John Shelby Spong's *Why Christianity Must Change or Die*—to a Sunday school class. They stopped reading it early on, once Spong argues that none of the miraculous events—the virgin birth, the miracles, a literal resurrection—are historically true. I kept reading, though, and I was intrigued by Spong's argument for why Jesus was divine. He said that Jesus met every person he encountered with unconditional love, and such a life simply cannot be human. Spong knows Jesus through his love.

The early church struggled with this idea, though, as the passage from Acts shows. Peter is recounting his encounter with Cornelius and his vision of God's making all of the unclean animals clean. Peter breaks countless Jewish commandments when he goes to Cornelius's house, and he ends by baptizing everyone there, welcoming them into the Christian faith. The church was still struggling with the idea of whether or not Gentiles could become Christians, so this scene is significant in that it is a clear welcome to outsiders by Jesus's most visible disciple, expanding Christianity to all people. Jesus's love is more powerful than the boundaries the church had set on who could and couldn't get in.

The church has a history of trying to keep certain groups out. For hundreds of years, the color of people's skin automatically prevented them from joining a church (or at least particular churches; there were other churches for those people), and the church was wrong to do so. Church leadership allowed women to join churches, but they kept women from any sort of leadership roles, and the church was wrong to do so. Race and gender are not problems the church has solved, but we have at least begun to improve there. Unfortunately, many churches now use sexual orientation or gender identity as another litmus test for who they allow in (or allow fully in), and the church is wrong to do so. Also, many churches do not adjust their physical buildings in a way that make them accessible to all people, regardless of their ability, and the church is wrong to do so.

In fact, such limitations are not simply wrong; they are antithetical to true Christianity. They go against this basic, new commandment that Jesus gives the disciples and us. When the author of I John talks about the spirit of the antichrist, these limitations are exactly what he has in mind. He echoes the gospel of John in pointing out that we should love one another because Christ loved us, but he also says that "whoever does not love does not know God." Such exclusionary behavior is evidence that we do not know God; it is antichristian. If the world will know we are Christians by our love, every time we close the door—literally and metaphorically—on someone, the world knows we are not Christians.

Peter finally realized that God's love went beyond the boundaries of Jew and Gentile. We have slowly learned that it goes beyond race and gender, and we are still slowly learning that. We are just beginning to learn that it transcends ability, sexual orientation, and gender identity. God loved us when others said we should be kept out. We must now love others, not as we love ourselves (that's way too easy), but as God loved us.

Questions for Reflection or Discussion:

How has the church struggled with who it should accept, historically and recently? How can we move beyond tolerance to truly loving everyone as a child of God?

How can the church be more open and welcoming today? What boundaries do we need to cross?

When the Spirit Moves

Sixth Sunday of Easter

John 14:15–21
Acts 10:34–48

PEOPLE IN THE PROGRESSIVE Christian tradition tend to have real difficulties talking about the Holy Spirit, given the associations with the Pentecostal tradition and spiritual gifts. We have often seen the Spirit misused to justify people's claims to speak for God when they are simply using emotionalism to manipulate people. While there are numerous cases of people in the Pentecostal tradition who do connect with the Spirit in meaningful ways and use those connections to truly help others, those examples seldom show up outside of the particular places where they occur. Some of us may have even grown up in churches where the leadership used the Spirit as an excuse for oppression, enforcing supposed rules and regulations that had no biblical basis with the claim that the Spirit had given them a particular message. In the same way that people use God's name as an excuse for outright evil, some churches and leaders have used the Spirit to defend their particular view of Christianity, often for their own ends, rather than to proclaim the good news of the kingdom.

If we're honest, though, some of us in the progressive tradition are simply bothered by the lack of control the Spirit often represents. There's a reason many of our churches joke about forming committees for even the smallest situations, as we seem incapable of acting quickly or without long periods of reflection (or whatever we want to call it). We might include more contemporary songs in our worship, but only a few of us are comfortable clapping along with them.

There is a place for the Spirit within our tradition, though, a way to see the Spirit moving that goes beyond the exaggerated stereotype of Pentecostalism. In Jesus's promise to send the Spirit after he has gone, he says that he will give the disciples (and us) an advocate. That word gets translated a number of ways, including *helper* and *comforter*, showing that the Spirit serves multiple roles. The Greek word seems to come closer to the way we think of the latter two, as it literally means *beside-caller*, which leads some versions to use *consoler*.

However, *advocate* is a popular translation because of the idea from legal settings, where the advocate is one who stands beside people charged with the crime and attempts to defend them. Thus, we often think of the Spirit as standing beside us in some way, defending us. One of the traditional readings of this verse, then, is that the Spirit stands beside us when we encounter God to defend us for our sinfulness, or even that the Spirit stands with us and helps us know what to say to defend our faith when we cannot do so ourselves. While both of those readings might work, that keeps the focus on ourselves, not on other people. They essentially argue that the Spirit's role is in some way to advocate for us, while it makes more sense that the Spirit is an advocate for other people. Granted, the Spirit does comfort and console us, as the Spirit reminds us that God is with us through the most difficult times. Those roles are important, and we should not ignore them when we think about the Spirit's purpose.

However, the Spirit can also advocate for other people whom we overlook or ignore. The Spirit takes on this role in the story from Acts, as the Spirit moves Peter to accept the Gentiles as fellow Christians. Peter has already had the dream declaring animals that Jewish law deemed unclean to be clean, and the Spirit has moved Cornelius to send for Peter. Here, Peter preaches the gospel to Cornelius and his household, and the Spirit makes it clear that the Gentiles are just as worthy of receiving that message as anyone else is, a radical notion to the Jewish Christians who were "astounded."

Peter does not get to this realization on his own. He needs a dream about clean or unclean foods, a messenger, and the response from Cornelius and his family to ultimately declare that Gentiles are equally welcome in the kingdom of God. He will also ultimately take that message back to the church at Jerusalem, beginning a change in the future of the church, leading to the worldwide spread of Christianity. Without the Spirit, none of these actions happen, and the church remains a small, closed group of believers in Israel. The Spirit, then, works through various means. First, the dream is a direct communication to Peter; second, the messenger is an outside person who has to come into Peter's life, and he has to respond to that message in an affirmative manner; last, the response of those around Peter, both Gentiles and Jews, communicates a new idea to Peter. All of these approaches are ones that still manifest themselves in the church today through the work of the Spirit.

We hear directly from the Spirit, whether through Bible study, reading, prayer, worship, service, music, or a variety of other means. Something in us begins to shift, and we have the first thought that there may be more to the good news than we originally thought. Someone outside of our traditional way of thinking comes into our lives, whether through a physical person or a movie, show, song, video, book, billboard, view of nature (this list could be as long as one of these entire reflections). We see other people acting in the world, whether through protests or politics, writing or reading, or just interacting with others. Any or all of these move us to realize we have been ignoring a person, a group of people, an area of the world, a political problem, a failing in ourselves, and, when we are at our best, they change us to be more like the people God wants us to be.

The Spirit is not advocating for us here, but for others, almost always those on the margins of our world and our churches. The Spirit tells us to provide better access to our buildings for those who have different abilities and needs than others of us. The Spirit tells heterosexuals to work for political rights for those who wish to marry members of their same sex. The Spirit tells cisgender people to include those who do not feel at home in the gender they were born into. The Spirit tells white males to walk beside people of color and women as societal constructions work to oppress them. The Spirit is still an advocate, still working to reform us and this world, still trying to bring the kingdom into here and now. We just have to listen to see where the Spirit is pushing us to go next.

Questions for Reflection or Discussion:

What are ways the Spirit has moved you to do something or become different in some way?

Where can we still see the need for the Spirit to move us, both locally and globally?

Looking in the Right Place

Ascension Day

Luke 24:44–53
Acts 1:1–11

T HESE TWO PASSAGES DETAILING the ascension, though probably written by the same author, give two slightly different accounts of Jesus's
ascension into heaven. In the gospel of Luke, Jesus sums up his role as Messiah and lays out the purpose of the church, promising power to help them
with their work. He then ascends to heaven while blessing them, leading
the disciples to return to Jerusalem, to the temple to praise God.

In Acts, the general structure is the same, though, in this account, the
disciples are more active, asking if Jesus will fulfill the traditional role of the
Messiah, showing that they still expect some sort of political revolution. Jesus
shifts the question (as he almost always does) away from that idea to their
spreading the word about his ministry. The other main difference in the Acts
account is that two men in white appear and ask the disciples why they're
looking up to heaven. Though the passage ends here, the next few verses do
tell us that the disciples returned to Jerusalem, but not to the temple; instead,
they go back to the upper room and choose a replacement for Judas.

Modern readers tend to question the historicity of this story, as it
seems the least believable of the post-resurrection stories, that Jesus simply
ascends into heaven. Instead, as with some of the other stories, people read
it more metaphorically than literally. In the gospel passage, then, it becomes
a representation of how the disciples felt after Jesus's departure, that they finally see what they are supposed to do after Jesus's death. The Acts account,
though, adds another reading with the appearance of the two men in white
and has something else to say to contemporary readers, as well.

Rather than ending this section with the disciples actively returning to Jerusalem, praising God, as the gospel passage does, the author of Acts shows us the main group of Jesus's followers doing nothing but staring up into the sky. As with so many of the stories involving the disciples, they are left as mere spectators, unable (or unwilling) to truly participate in the action of the story, needing someone to describe the importance of the event to them. They need one more bit of prodding before they are able to take up the charge Jesus has just put upon them.

The problem is that they're still looking up in the sky for guidance for their next move. While the Bible, especially the book of Acts, encourages the disciples and all people of faith to look toward Jesus for guidance, the passage here doesn't imply that's what the disciples were doing. Instead, they were looking to heaven, wondering when Jesus would descend and continue the work he was doing. If people look for guidance, it's because they wants help in doing the work they need to do; the disciples are looking instead for Jesus to continue the doing. Even their return to the upper room to select a new disciple (who's never mentioned again) seems more like a bureaucratic move rather than their beginning to carry out Jesus's charge.

One way we can read this passage, then, is simply that we often look to God or Jesus to do the work we should be doing. Whenever people have a need, we tell them we'll pray for the situation, but we don't take action to actually make that situation better. When we need to correct something in our lives, we ask God to do the work of changing us rather than putting in the time and discipline to work for that change, asking for help instead. Rather than asking God to do whatever it is that needs doing, we need to take on the role of the body of Christ and act as his hands and feet to minister to a world that needs a great deal of help.

While that reading is true and helpful and a good reminder of how often we push the responsibility away from ourselves and onto God, we also look in the wrong place in another way. Rather than looking to God or to ourselves to right the wrongs of this world, we often look to politics or organizations or companies. Instead of actively seeking to care for others, to make difficult choices to do what is right, we ask people outside of ourselves to do that work for us, relieving us of the responsibility. We'll write checks and cast our votes, but we won't actually do the work that needs doing.

While we need people to write checks to worthwhile organizations, and we definitely need to be involved in the political process, those actions will not solve the real problems of this world. Instead, we need people who will work with those around them to make the world a better place. While we work to provide government programs that will help the poorest among us have access to quality food, the church must also work to provide that food for those in each community. While we petition the government to end programs that perpetuate systemic racism, we also must be intentional about crossing racial lines in our personal lives and as a church. While we encourage our lawmakers and justices to uphold the rights of the most marginal in our society, whether based on ability or gender or race or sexual orientation or gender identity, we must go outside of our church buildings and interact with those who don't feel welcome there.

We're looking in the wrong places when we look toward politics or non-profits or corporations to solve what is a moral and ethical problem. The only way to truly change that is to change people's hearts. Jesus doesn't tell his disciples to go out and found organizations or vote; he tells them to be his witnesses throughout the world. We need to take Jesus's radical message of inclusion into our workplaces and communities and homes, living it out on a daily basis, all while working through the other spheres of this world, as they are part of our charge, as well. We just can't expect them to be the solution; for that, we have to look in the mirror.

Questions for Reflection or Discussion:

Where does the church need to be more creative in the local community to solve larger problems?

What are the barriers that keep the church from doing so? How can we overcome those?

Nobody Likes Me

Seventh Sunday of Easter

John 17:11b–19

T HIS PASSAGE FROM THE gospel of John, part of the ending of Jesus's farewell address to his disciples just before he is arrested, is one of those passages those of us who grew up in the evangelical tradition heard on a regular basis. Our ministers and church leaders told us that the world would hate us, as Jesus says here, and that we did not belong to the world. The reasons they gave us, though, often centered around ways we very purposefully chose not to fit with the world. Depending on the tradition and particular church, we might have avoided secular music or movies or television shows, listening to and watching only Christian media. We might even have skipped our high school proms or New Year's Eve parties or Halloween celebrations, possibly even celebrating Christmas as nothing more than a secular holiday, if at all. And, clearly, we wouldn't drink or smoke or have sex outside of marriage, as those were sins the Bible undeniably condemned.

It was the hatred by the world, though, that some churches wanted to emphasize. It wasn't just that we refrained from participating in worldly activities, as we called them; instead, we wanted the world to know we were different than they were, so we proudly announced our differences, whether at school or work or even in our churches. We expected the world to hate us, though *hate* is a strong word for the reactions we received; it was mainly puzzlement or pity that people gave in response to hearing what we didn't participate in.

The emphasis was always on what we didn't do, as is clear from the list of activities we refused to participate in. We defined ourselves by negative differences, how we didn't drink or participate in Halloween or listen to music that promoted behaviors we couldn't condone. We were modern day Pharisees, essentially, defining ourselves by the rules and regulations we kept and attempted to impose on others. When the world didn't understand our choices, we felt we were living a life Jesus would approve of, as he clearly states the world will hate us.

However, Jesus didn't live a life based on saying no to certain behaviors, and he doesn't encourage such an approach here. He ate with tax collectors and prostitutes, and I'm sure he heard more language there than we did when we were in high school, surrounded by the sinners we were trying not to associate with. He allowed a woman to wash his feet with her tears and hair, an act religious leaders would have seen almost on a level with having sex, as Jewish men and women did not touch in public. In fact, many scholars argue that the woman was a prostitute, given that she was wearing her hair down and touching a man in public. Regardless, Jesus accepted invitations to gather with anyone who wanted to be around him, and he engaged in behaviors his world would have condemned.

In fact, Jesus's world did hate him, as he says here, but it's not for the reasons those ministers and church leaders proposed for us. It was because Jesus angered them by not following their rules and regulations, the ones that separated people from one another. He healed Romans and Syro-Phoenicians, as well as Jews; he touched women and the dead; his followers included a tax collector, as well as women; he healed on the Sabbath. He continually acted out of love, not out of fear of breaking man-made rules that did nothing more than reinforce the power structure of the religious leaders.

He also spoke out against the hypocrisy he saw in the religious structure of his day. He turned over the tables in the temple, disrupting an economic system that preyed on the poor in the name of God. He pointed out how the scribes and Pharisees manipulated their own rules and regulations to benefit themselves while penalizing those beneath them. He showed how the religious leaders turned religion into a performance, with their public prayers and overly dramatized times of fasting, wanting to act out a faith that wasn't genuine, while the widow who gave what little she had truly embodied the kingdom. However, he acted, even here, out of love, knowing that many of the religious leaders truly sought to follow God, knowing that they, too, could hear his message, if they had ears to hear.

Of course, the major figures in Jesus's world were the Romans, the people who ultimately put him to death. He spoke out about real power, not the political power the Romans enforced on the Jews and so many other people. He explained and illustrated that love would ultimately win over violence, that those who live by the sword will die by it, as well. Yet he did so, even while healing a Centurion's servant and praising the faith of the Centurion in the process.

In all of these actions, we see Jesus acting, not from a place of denial, but from action, seeking to make the world a better place not through telling people what they shouldn't do, but modeling what we should. The world hated Jesus, not because he set out to show the world that refraining from sinful actions would earn their scorn, but because he showed the emptiness in the lives of those who put their faith in what the world holds dear: money, power, division, possessions, violence, revenge, selfishness. We don't want to see ourselves as we truly are, as people who look out only for ourselves and will do whatever we need to do to protect what we value.

Jesus showed people a different way, a way of unconditional love and grace and acceptance, which leads to true peace, and such a life threatens people. Whenever great leaders—from Martin Luther King, Jr. to Socrates to Oscar Romero—have tried to remind people of injustice, of how focusing only on ourselves lead to a world where the majority of people suffer without our seeing them, the world has hated those people and sought to silence them. Jesus wants us to understand that the world will hate us, not because of the music we choose not to listen to, but because our lives should remind people of what is truly important; our lives should model justice and peace and unconditional love. We might make people uncomfortable, but we will also show people the possibilities of a life of faith and justice.

Questions for Reflection or Discussion:

What are ways our lives should make others uncomfortable, possibly even leading people to hate us?

How can we put forth the positive actions of Jesus in today's society, as opposed to becoming like the Pharisees and focusing on what we shouldn't do?

The Wind Blows All the Walls Down

Day of Pentecost

Acts 2:1–21
Genesis 11:1–9
Numbers 11:24–30

T HE DAY OF PENTECOST pairs well with the Genesis story of the Tower of Babel, as each centers around language as a way we divide or unite ourselves. We live in a time where money can flow freely across national boundaries, but people cannot, a time where we use our nationalities and our languages to keep us apart rather than bring us together. These two stories, then, are just the right stories for our time.

In the Tower of Babel, God seems threatened by what people can do when they have a common language, as if building a tower is some representation of the ability to overthrow divinity. In fact, what's puzzling about this story is how God is bothered by the unity of humanity. It's fairly clear that this story from our early history is an explanation of why there are different languages, but the presentation of God makes less sense to us. In an attempt to understand why people from different places speak differently, the storyteller puts the blame on God, not on humanity, as if people would be unified if only God hadn't separated us by giving us these different languages.

Anyone who has had any real interactions with people knows that language is only one of many aspects of our natures we use to divide us. Instead of viewing this story as one about God's confusing humanity, then, perhaps it's more useful to look at it to see what we can learn about humanity. Even when this group does come together, they do so only to build a city and a tower, the purpose of which is unclear. It could be a tower that they would use to defend the city from whomever might think of invading it, reminding us that, though these people are united behind a common goal, there are others outside this city who don't share that goal.

The tower could also be simply what they say it is, a way to make their name. If they are creating the tower as nothing more than a status symbol, then there must be some people outside the city they want to impress in some way. Even when we have a group of people coming together for a common purpose, we create one group that is inside and another that is outside. God's scattering of these people is not what divides them; there are already divisions in the world. The different languages just make those differences more visible.

The passage from Acts, which details the Day of Pentecost, serves as the opposite of the Tower of Babel story, it seems. Those people who were once so divided by language now are miraculously united in hearing the gospel story, as Jesus's followers are able to speak in all the languages of the known world. These mostly poor, uneducated disciples of Jesus are now able to speak languages they had only heard in passing in major cities, such as Jerusalem, and they all share the same message of God's love. They are united in language and in purpose, taking us back to before Babel.

The Pentecost story doesn't end there, though. It's not just a story about language any more than the Babel story is. Instead, we hear Peter's speech to the crowd (which gets a chuckle every year when he defends the lack of drunkenness simply by pointing out that it's nine o'clock in the morning) explaining why the Pentecost event is happening. He quotes the prophet Joel's account of God's pouring out of his Spirit on his followers, though Joel connects such an event to the "last days," which seems not to be the case on Pentecost.

In that passage, though, the prophet Joel goes beyond the divisions of language to talk about other divisions the Spirit would erase: gender, age, and freedom status. He says that men and women will prophesy, as will the old and the young, the free and the slave. When the Spirit comes, Joel (and, thus, Peter) says that everyone will have the ability to speak the words of God, ending with Peter's declaration that "everyone who calls on the name of the Lord will be saved."

We can see the same approach in the lesser-known passage from Numbers when the Spirit settles on Eldad and Medad, enabling them to prophesy, though they are not in the supposedly proper place. As has happened so many times throughout history, Joshua (essentially the right hand man of Moses, one of the most powerful people among the Israelites) encourages Moses to stop them from doing so. Moses, though, knowing the power and purpose of God responds that he wishes that all the Lord's people would be prophets and speak God's word.

Throughout the world and the church's histories, we have sought to silence certain people, whether because of their gender or age or freedom status or because of their sexual orientation or gender identity or race or ability. The church's leaders, like Joshua, have said that only the right people in the right place were free to speak God's words, whether officially (ordained as ministers) or unofficially (in the church or world at large). Time after time, though, we see God breaking through our created divisions, reminding us that the kingdom of God is larger than what we can imagine, that, as Peter says, everyone is welcome here, and, as Moses and Joel say, everyone should be able to speak the words of God.

Pentecost is certainly about God's ability to break down our national and ethnic boundaries, those imaginary lines we draw on maps and enforce as if they are real. But Pentecost is about so much more than that. It's about God trying, one more time, as dramatically as possible, to tell us to put aside all, not some, of our differences because of God's message of radical love and inclusion. When we do so, as with Babel, there is no telling what we can accomplish in this world.

Questions for Reflection or Discussion:

Historically, what barriers has the church set up to keep people from speaking the words of God, and what barriers still remain in the church?

What are barriers or divisions society creates, and how can the church help bring them down?

Not Going It Alone

Trinity Sunday

John 3:1–17
Isaiah 6:1–8

THE READINGS FOR TRINITY Sunday are not what one would expect, as we don't see a passage that tries to lay out the doctrine of the trinity. That's probably because there aren't any, as the trinity is not a concept that's explicitly laid out in the Bible. Those who put the King James Version together inserted a verse that did clearly lay out the concept (I John 5:7), as they wanted at least one verse that would clearly establish the trinity as a doctrine with scriptural support. Otherwise, when people want to prove the trinity exists as they envision it, they cobble together passages that say that Jesus is one with the Father and the Spirit of God moved over the waters, and, see, they're all one. It's the theological equivalent of transitive relations in math (if A>B and B>C, then A>C).

We need people who focus on theology and doctrine, certainly, but, for most of us, the idea of the trinity doesn't affect our daily (or yearly, actually) lives. If someone came along tomorrow and definitively disproved the idea of the trinity, almost none of us would notice any difference in what we believed or how we lived our lives. We would probably even keep baptizing people in the name of the Father, the Son, and the Holy Spirit, partly because we've done so for hundreds of years, but partly because it's not as if those three entities would have ceased to be important or stop existing.

It's what those three things do that matter, not the fact that they're one or not. Thus, on Trinity Sunday, we don't get a list of verses that, in some way, tries to prove the doctrine of the trinity. Instead, we get passages that remind us of what God, however we want to think about God, whether in multiple forms/persons or in one, does, and, accordingly, what we should do. In the passage from John, where Nicodemus is sneaking at night to see Jesus, there are two actions that God performs that change our lives, which leads to the passage from Isaiah that lays out what we should do.

As befits a Pharisee, Nicodemus and Jesus do have a theological discussion about what we now call being born again (though that phrase has, unfortunately, become as political as it is religious), which does lead to a discussion about the Spirit. As is almost always the case, the person who's supposed to be knowledgeable about God ends up confused after talking with Jesus (especially in the gospel of John, where Jesus tends to be much more abstract and wordy), leaving Jesus to summarize the important parts at the end of the discussion. There's a reason many of us grew up memorizing John 3:16 and not one of the earlier verses about being born of water and the Spirit.

It's interesting that the verse that has become the most popular verse about Christianity, supposedly the one that sums up the gospel, is one that, at least according to this gospel, Jesus spoke to one person in a secretive meeting at night. If this idea were so important, one would think that Jesus would have found other occasions to say such a remark more explicitly. After all, this verse clearly lays out that God loved humanity so much that God was willing to give Jesus to us or for us, all to save us from perishing. This verse is the core of the dominant view of Jesus's role as the sacrifice for the sins of the world, the sacrificial view of the atonement.

However, that's not the only way to read this verse. There's nothing at all in this verse about Jesus's being sent to die for the sins of humanity, just that God sent Jesus to keep people from perishing. The way that Jesus does that is through giving us a model of how to live our lives, through his giving us teachings to encourage us to live lives focused on others, not ourselves. The reason Jesus doesn't need to go around proclaiming this verse on a regular basis is because Jesus lived it out and proclaimed God's radically inclusive love with how he interacted with everyone he met. If people never read this verse, but read about how Jesus lived otherwise, they would certainly come to the same conclusion.

The following verse, the one most people forget about, simply reinforces this idea (that word *Indeed* is a great word to show us that it is repeating the idea from the previous verse). God doesn't want to condemn people, and that's definitely not why God wanted Jesus to live and teach as he did. Instead, God wants people to see the life they could have if they would love and forgive as Jesus did. Unfortunately, many people have taken John 3:16 to divide the world into those who are in (i.e. those who believe as they do) and those who are out, clearly condemning entire swaths of the world rather easily.

The job, then, of Christians, is to take that message of radically inclusive love and forgiveness and grace to a world that desperately needs it, a world torn by divisions and war and hatred and greed. Like Isaiah, we know that we're not worthy to take on such a task, not because we don't measure up to some standard God has laid out, but because we are flawed and fallible creatures, and we will not live up the ideas we want others to embrace. We will fail to forgive the person who has hurt us; we will fall short of loving those who need it; we will forget to offer grace to someone who truly needs it. We will feel like a hypocrite, someone with unclean lips, because we tell others to love and forgive, while we don't do so ourselves.

However, God touches us with a live coal and cleanses us. God takes away our guilt, if we will accept that forgiveness. God forgives and forgets our sins, if we will accept that grace. God takes us as we are, but loves us enough to want us to be better, if we will accept that love. Because we live in that state of grace, we respond, as Isaiah did, "Here am I; send me," because we want others to know what a life fully lived can feel like. And, as many ministers say at the end of their services, we don't do this work alone. We go with the grace our Lord Jesus Christ, the love of God, and the fellowship of the Holy Spirit. We have three or one or somebody going with us, no matter what our theological understanding of that idea might be.

Questions for Reflection or Discussion:

What ideas do we have about the trinity, and how do they both help and hinder us in the work of the kingdom?

What are ways we use verses like John 3:16 to exclude people, and how can we use them to help others feel welcome?

Breaking the Law

Second Sunday After Pentecost

Mark 2:23–28
Deuteronomy 5:12–15

JESUS WAS A RATHER notorious rule breaker. He broke a number of them, and he did so often. He healed on the Sabbath and in the synagogue; he talked to women in public (Samaritans, no less); he touched the dead, as he was healing them; he didn't wash his hands before he ate (no wonder his mother worried about him); his disciples didn't fast; and on and on. It's easy to read the gospels and see Jesus as someone who was nothing more than a scofflaw, an adolescent thumbing his nose at an out-of-date approach to Judaism. Perhaps if church leaders presented him this way, fewer teenagers would rebel by leaving the church; Jesus could be their role model rather than someone to rebel against.

Such a presentation of him, though, would be a caricature. It's true that Jesus broke the rules on a regular basis, but he wasn't behaving like a moody teenager who just wanted to show his parents (that would be complicated, in this case) that he was his own person or a college student who just wants to stick it to the man (though he did), even quoting scripture back to the Pharisees to prove his point. We have to reconcile this picture of Jesus with the one who talks about fulfilling the law and the prophets, the one who reminds us that not even the smallest part of the law will pass away. In fact, when Jesus responds to the question of the greatest commandment, he doesn't make up something new; he quotes from the Torah, reminding his hearers that they've already been given the greatest commandment(s); they now have to live out the love that God has already shown them.

Jesus is taking the same approach in this passage from the gospel of Mark, as he is not creating some new approach to the Sabbath; instead, he's trying to remind the Pharisees of what's truly important to God. The Pharisees have a narrow view of the Sabbath, having parsed the original commandment over centuries to develop specific rules of what constitutes *work*, a seemingly simple term that they have admitted is much more complicated than it seems (and it is). We often blame the Pharisees, but they have a point here. It's easy to say that we should not work on the Sabbath, but we then start getting twisted around what work actually is: if someone enjoys gardening, can they weed on the Sabbath? if someone loves small engine repair, can they rebuild an engine on the Sabbath?

The problem with these questions and the point the Pharisees raise is that they miss the point of the original commandment. We and the Pharisees are trying to understand what we can and cannot get away with; we want the rule to be as specific as possible, so we know exactly what we can and cannot do. If anyone questions whether this approach is simply human, rather than Pharisaical, just talk to anyone around tax time and see the questions people ask then, or simply be a teacher and try to give any type of assignment.

The point of the original commandment is not to limit what people can do, but to free them to worship and delight in God with gratitude. We will naturally fill our lives with work we feel has to get done, especially in our society, but even in the time when the Israelites lived by the ten commandments, when there were always animals or crops that could use their attention. God wants the Israelites to take care of themselves and their households and their animals and the land, so God tells them to take a day off every week. Otherwise, they are nothing more than the slaves they were in Egypt, when work ruled their lives.

When we are free to make our own decisions, it is natural that we would want to work on what is ours, to make it better. We then, though, become a slave to whatever that work is, whether it's tending to animals or saving money to make the bottom line look a bit better to planting crops to responding to emails from customers about the product we want them to buy. The Israelites were in danger of shifting from being slaves in Egypt to being slaves to their work, in the same way that we often enslave ourselves to whatever work we do to make our living. We even have important reasons—saving for a house; we need a new car; kids need to attend college—for all of that work, but we are still enslaved.

Jesus wants to remind the Pharisees, the disciples, and us that there is yet another way of being enslaved. By working so hard to make sure we are not enslaved to our work, taking off that one day a week every day, every year, we can become enslaved to the rule itself, causing damage to ourselves or to those around us. The disciples are simply hungry, as they are walking from one place to another, so they pluck some grain and begin to eat it. They clearly have not prepared meals ahead of time, as would have been the custom, so they want to give themselves enough sustenance for the walk. They could keep the rule that God laid out to help people take care of themselves or they could break the rule and actually take care of themselves.

Jesus argues that the original commandment was designed for the good of all humans, not as some arbitrary rule God has given people for no particular reason. The Pharisees know the rules quite well, but they have forgotten the motivation behind them. Jesus, time and time again, will say that God cares more about humanity than God does the rules. Any commandments God ever gave were to help us live with ourselves and all of our failings, both within ourselves and when we are in community.

This same recognition is often lacking in churches today, as people focus on what is proper or appropriate, following rules that once benefited humanity, but now cause us to dehumanize ourselves or others. We tell people not to work on the Sabbath—ignoring the reality of those who have to work two or three jobs (or even just the one they're thankful to have)—and come to church, as if that were more important than providing food for themselves or a family. We encourage people to overcommit to the church, to work one more day a week, rather than providing them a place and a community where they can find rest and nourishment, encouraging them to find balance in their lives by both serving and being served.

Jesus points out that we need to work when we need to work and we need to rest when we need to rest. God wants us to take that time for ourselves or our families, no matter what others might think or what rules people create. God gives us rules to help us live better lives, not so that we can focus on ourselves, but so that we can focus on making the world a better place, even when we have to break the rules to do so.

Questions for Reflection or Discussion:

What are rules we now try to follow so exactly they end up hurting us more than helping us?

How can the church provide a better model of a balance between rest and work than it has done historically?

How to Stand Up

Third Sunday After Pentecost

Mark 3:20–35
Genesis 3:8–15

E ARLY IN THE GOSPEL of Mark, people are not receiving Jesus's message well. People are saying that he has lost his mind; the scribes are saying that he's possessed; and his family now comes to intervene, hoping to get him to stop teaching and healing. Jesus, not surprisingly, stands up to all of these groups, pointing out that casting out demons shouldn't convince anyone that he's possessed by the devil, and he claims that people who do the will of God are his true family. We take it for granted that Jesus is going to assert his authority and the truth of his message, as that's what Jesus does.

We often forget, in our day to day lives, how difficult it is to hold views or perform actions that those around us do not share, whether they are something relatively small, such as how we eat (if we're vegetarian or vegan), or a major life choice, such as protesting an issue we disagree with (such as the death penalty), even being willing to go to jail for it. No matter if we're thirteen or thirty or sixty, it is especially difficult when the people who are encouraging us to live like everyone else or accept what others believe are our family members. We would expect them, of all people, to support our decision, yet they are often the ones who push back against us the most.

If we're honest, most of the time, we do go along with what others want or say, keeping many of our thoughts or actions private. If we're sitting at lunch with co-workers, we know it's easier to sit silently when someone makes a racist comment or joke; if we're around the dinner table, we can easily excuse our father or aunt's statement about immigrants because that's just how they are; if we see a news story about a politician voting for a bill we disagree with, we can talk about how we don't have time to write or call them, as we're all busy, and we already voted, which should be enough.

Jesus, though, sets out a different model, one in which we take the risk of making unpopular comments, of speaking out where we see injustice, even if it gets us labeled as crazy or possessed, or just gets our family to come after us to try to quiet us down. He knows it's difficult, but he also knows it's what should set Christians apart, as we have different goals than most people. We're more concerned about love and grace and justice than we are about making other people happy when they should be uncomfortable about their actions.

However, what truly sets Jesus apart is why he behaves the way he does. The ending of the passage from the gospel of Mark often bothers readers for the way Jesus treats his family. He seems to separate himself from them, breaking away to say that, because they don't agree with him, they are no longer his family. Early church history, though, shows that such a break didn't actually occur, as both Mary, his mother, and James, his brother, became leaders in the church. He's not arguing here that his family isn't important, just that his family is broader than what people imagine. He's not breaking away from his family; he's including more people in it. Jesus doesn't rebel against the norms of his culture because he hates it or the people with whom he disagrees; he does so because he loves people.

The passage from Genesis shows the opposite of Jesus, as Adam and Eve blame each other and the serpent for their actions, trying to pass the blame to someone else. They take the problem and look outside of themselves for the cause of it, turning against one another as soon as they begin to get themselves into trouble. Rather than looking at themselves as the cause and looking at each other as people who deserve grace and forgiveness, they protect themselves and blame others.

The problems that occur in society don't simply happen because of what other people do; they happen because of who we are, all of us. We can critique the ways in which capitalism oppresses the poor, perpetuating a cycle of poverty, which ultimately widens the gap between the haves and have nots, but we also have to admit that we are greedy people, seeking to protect ourselves and our families, watching our retirement plans closer than we do the income equality numbers. We can call out the various types of discrimination, both personal and systemic, we see, whether based on race, gender identity or sexual orientation, ability, or gender, but we also must notice when our friends are people who share our characteristics and often our politics, rather than crossing boundaries ourselves.

Of course, we should speak out against such injustices, but we must do so from a place of humility and love, remembering that, like Adam and Eve, we are flawed, as well. Otherwise, we become driven by pride or hate, despising those other people who are the cause of problems in society. Near the end of his essay, "Notes of a Native Son," James Baldwin realizes that he was in danger of going down this path in his fight against injustice, especially racial inequality. He writes, "This fight begins, however, in the heart and it now had been laid to my charge to keep my own heart free of hatred and despair." He knows that it is too easy to turn the desire for justice into the hatred of those who stop such progress, so he warns himself and us not to pursue that route.

The way we find the courage to stand up to injustice is not through a hatred of those who perpetuate such practices. Instead, it is through knowing that we participate in injustice ourselves, that we are fallible people who often fall short of our own ideals, but who remember that God loves us anyway, as God did Adam and Eve, and as God does everyone, including those we hope to convince to change their behavior. Jesus knows this truth about humanity, so he is able to stand up to his family, the religious establishment, and the people talking about him. We, too, can do the same, confident that God, too, seeks justice through love and grace.

Questions for Reflection or Discussion:

When are times you or your church did not speak up against some sort of injustice? Or what are issues where we should speak up more often?

What can the church do to help give people the support they need to stand up to the wrongs we see in society?

Not What We Want to Hear

Fourth Sunday After Pentecost

Matthew 10:34–42
Jeremiah 28:5–9

A T A TIME WHERE we have multiple wars in the Middle East and Africa, not to mention tensions in Asia (especially North Korea) that could lead to war, civil unrest in parts of South America, and the recent invasion of Ukraine—wars or rumors of war on almost every continent—the last thing we want to hear from Jesus is that he doesn't come to bring peace. Christians for centuries have proclaimed him as the Prince of Peace, and they and we have prayed for peace year after year. Yet here we have Jesus, speaking quite clearly, saying that he doesn't come to bring peace, but a sword, the synechdocal representation for strife.

Not only does Jesus not bring peace, he's going to separate families, that institution of Western Christianity, with marriage serving as a sacrament, traditionally undergirding the family. Rather than uniting people to work against injustice, Jesus is actually going to separate families, turning them against one another, creating more conflict in a world already riddled with it. This Jesus doesn't sound like the one progressives or evangelicals talk about in the pulpit week after week; this Jesus might be one we can all agree we're not comfortable with, though perhaps for different reasons.

One way people explain this passage is through arguing that Jesus is not really talking about his bringing conflict to the world; instead, he is just pointing out that there will always be division, much in the same way he explained that there will always be poverty in the world. In the same way that that admission shouldn't keep us from working to end poverty, we should not stop working toward peace. The passage from Jeremiah seems to

118

support such a reading, as Jeremiah reminds Hananiah (his rival prophet, essentially, who told King Zedekiah what he wanted to hear) that any prophet who proclaims peace will be a true prophet only when such peace actually comes. It's clear Jeremiah doesn't think that's going to happen.

While it's true that Jesus and Jeremiah recognize human nature and the truth that there will always be division, and while it's true that neither of them would argue that we should stop working for peace because of that recognition, Jesus is saying something different here, as is Jeremiah. Both of them are talking about proclaiming the truth and the results of doing so.

Jeremiah is clearer in the passages surrounding this one, but even here, one can hear the mockery in his voice, as he tells Hananiah that the prophet who proclaims peace will be the true prophet when it occurs. He knows, though, the previous prophets have warned countries of famine and war and suffering because they were disobeying God. Jeremiah tells people, whether it's a king or another prophet, the harsh truth about humanity, even if it means he is ridiculed. Jeremiah didn't even want to be a prophet; he tried to resist his calling, as he knew what it would entail. Telling the truth doesn't gain one popularity, whether in ancient Israel or in the contemporary Western world.

That's exactly the point Jesus is trying to get his followers to understand. Earlier in the chapter, he has sent his disciples out to preach, and he wants them to know that most people will not accept their message. Even within their own families, people will shun them, turn away from them, cast them out, even disown them, all because Jesus's message is one they refuse to hear. As much as possible, he wants them to be prepared for the attacks, the vitriol, that will come from people who disagree with them. Carrying Jesus's message is carrying a cross, which will lead to suffering and banishment, even death for many of Jesus's followers, though they don't know that yet.

Of course, it's difficult for us in the twenty-first century Western world to understand such a point. We have to manufacture persecutions on Christians in America, creating such supposed crises as "The War on Christmas" to talk about how the secular, pagan world treats true believers. There is no modern equivalent of carrying our cross because most of our lives, as far as expressing our religion in America goes, are smooth and unbothered. We can go to church whenever we want, read the Bible, pray, even stand on street corners and proclaim whatever we believe to be true, if we like. We don't understand what it means to carry a cross because we'll never have to, for which we should be thankful.

However, living the life Jesus calls us to does create conflict between people and especially within families because Jesus's message is still counter-cultural. When we question whether businesses should focus on the bottom line or on being productive members of a community, keeping jobs in small towns that are dying, even if it means lower profits, our friends or family members who help run that company will disagree with us. When we protest the prison-industrial complex, especially the move toward private prison companies more focused on profit than rehabilitation, our friends or family members who see that as their best option for employment will question our allegiance to them. When we argue that the systems of power—whether political or economic or even religious—consistently oppress those who are on the margins, whether because of income or race or ability or gender or sexual orientation or gender identity, our friends and family who benefit from those systems will condemn us, even call us un-American.

Jesus isn't talking about peace between nations in this passage or those divisions that will always occur because of human nature; he wants his disciples and us to know that truly living out a life of radical inclusivity and justice will cause division. There are consequences to speaking the truth, as Jeremiah understood; it is much easier to be the person telling those in power what they hope to hear. Jesus, though, calls us to a life of truth-telling, of saying what those who oppress don't want to hear, no matter the difficulties. Jesus was put to death for telling the truth. Few of us will be called on to do the same, but we have to be willing to take the consequences that do come, even losing those closest to us. Like Jeremiah, we might resist it, but, if we don't do it, no one else will.

Questions for Reflection or Discussion:

Where are places in society today where the church speaks unpopular truths, leading to division?

How do we manage those situations where our speaking about injustices alienates family and friends?

Being Neighborly

Fifth Sunday After Pentecost

Luke 10:25–37
Leviticus 19:9–18

T HE PARABLE OF THE Good Samaritan, as we have come to call this passage, is so pervasive in Western culture that even many people outside of the church know it, at least on some level. Even if they couldn't tell any plot point of the actual parable or who an actual Samaritan was, they could tell what people mean when they call someone a good Samaritan. There is even, in the world of recreational vehicles (RVs), a Good Sam club, which began with members promising to help travelers whenever they saw them in trouble (the club has now morphed into a type of AAA for RVs, though their logo still has a man with a halo over his head).

When we talk about this passage in church, we often focus on the question of how we should or shouldn't act out this parable today, discussing the realities of stopping for someone broken down on the highway, for example. This question is especially pertinent for those who would most likely be targets for people who pretend to be broken down, whether women, people with children, or the older members of congregations. We all explain that we understand why they wouldn't stop, and we try not to make them feel guilty.

We treat this parable as if it were a real story, not a parable Jesus is telling to answer the lawyer's question. *Parable* literally means "to throw beside of" in Greek, as it is simply a story used to illustrate a point, not the point itself. It's similar to an idea found in a Buddhist *koan*, that faith's version of a parable: there is an image of a man pointing to the moon, and the saying is that the finger is not the moon. Too often we focus on the finger rather than the moon, while the finger is nothing more than a means to get us to the moon.

In this case, the parable itself is not the point. The good Samaritan doesn't exist in reality; he is simply Jesus's creation to help the lawyer and crowd understand a much more important point. Before Jesus tells this story, the lawyer has asked what he must do to inherit eternal life. Jesus puts the question back to him (as he often does), and the lawyer answers correctly that he must love God and love his neighbor. When Jesus tells him he is correct, the author of Luke shows that the lawyer wanted "to justify himself." The lawyer knows what he should do, but he also knows that he's not doing it. In the stereotypical fashion of lawyers today, then, this lawyer looks for a loophole, wanting to know the exact meaning of *neighbor*.

Jesus's parable certainly illustrates the idea of who the lawyer's neighbor is, as the Samaritan is more of a neighbor to the person who was attacked than either the priest of Levite. The Samaritan crosses long-held ethnic divisions to help someone who probably despised him and his kind. He touches what might have been a dead body, as he didn't know the man was still alive until he checked on him. He then went well beyond what any listeners, ancient or contemporary, would expect him to do, taking the man to the inn, paying enough for whatever lodging and care he might need, with the promise of returning to make more payment, as well.

The Samaritan here is carrying out the role of neighbor as God laid it out in Leviticus, where the Israelites were told to love their neighbors (this passage also shows up in the lectionary on the Seventh Sunday After Epiphany) before. However, the religious leaders of Jesus's time would interpret that Leviticus passage to apply only to Israelites, save for the opening passage about harvesting their field, where they're specifically told to leave food for the alien. The rest of the passage (and the rest of their laws) applied to how to treat fellow Israelites, not anyone outside their community. Jesus, by using a Samaritan, points out that the religious leaders are missing the point of the Leviticus passage, as well, that the Samaritan in the story understands their own laws better than they do.

Jesus goes even further, though, with the inclusion of the Samaritan in this story. Most scholars argue that listeners in Jesus's time would have expected the third person who showed up to be an everyday Israelite. They would have understood why the priest and Levite passed the beaten man without stopping: he might have been dead, and the dead were unclean. The priest and the Levite were simply being cautious about not breaking their vows of cleanliness; an Israelite who was not among the religious leaders would have been more likely to help, as he had taken no such vows (though he would still have to go through the ritual to become clean again; it was simply less work and did not take him away from the religious duties the priest and Levite would have had to give up for a time).

Jesus is pointing out the hypocrisy of the religious leaders in that they put their vows of cleanliness above helping someone who desperately needed attention. They were following the literal interpretation of some of the laws, while clearly ignoring the intention of many of the other ones. The lawyer clearly knows the Levitical law, but he is unwilling to put it into practice, so Jesus tells a story of two religious leaders who do the same, then uses a Samaritan to show what true understanding of the law looks like. Jesus knows the lawyer is trying to justify his inaction, so Jesus shows him the true meaning of the law.

What Jesus wanted his followers and us to understand is how easy it is to justify our lack of action. When those of us in positions of privilege see racism or sexism or ableism or homophobia, it is easier to justify why we keep walking or stand aside and watch. When we notice economic inequalities in our society that do not prevent us from living the lifestyle we want, we create myths about bootstraps and hard work to explain why we don't work to end that injustice. We focus on a fictional story about someone else who came along and helped instead of looking at the lawyer, the one who might be more like us than we're willing to admit. Jesus gives us a role model in the Samaritan, certainly, but he is also warning us not to be like the lawyer, who spends his days standing around asking theoretical questions rather than acting on what he already knows.

Questions for Reflection or Discussion:

If we were telling this parable today, who would we put in the roles to illustrate the same ideas Jesus is trying to communicate?

What are issues or situations today where we try to justify our inaction?

Bringing the Kingdom

Sixth Sunday After Pentecost

Mark 5:21–43
Lamentations 3:22–33

WE OFTEN TALK ABOUT the passage from the gospel of Mark as more examples of Jesus's crossing boundaries, as we should. He touches a dead girl and does not condemn a woman who touches him, praising her for her faith instead, both of which would have been unexpected in his time. As he often does, Jesus shows compassion and love for those who are suffering, whether they are the father of a girl who has died or a woman who has suffered for as long as that girl lived. He treats them with the unfailing patience they need in their situation, even withstanding people's mocking his attempts to help, modeling the type of life those of us who try to follow Jesus should strive for.

That reading makes perfect sense, as it sums up so much about Jesus. We could find numerous other stories throughout the gospel accounts that match up with this image of Jesus, whether it's the healing of the widow's son, the conversation with the Samaritan woman at the well, or defending the woman caught in adultery. Nothing about these stories, as far as Jesus goes, surprises anyone who has read the gospels, as Jesus performs such actions time and time again. That consistency is the point here, as this story is not so much about Jesus's actions at this time, but how and why he had the chance to perform these actions at all.

Quite often, Jesus doesn't initiate the healings he performs; instead, people seek him out in one way or another, whether they are blind and sitting on the side of the road crying out for him or sending someone to find him to see if he will help. In this case, we have two people who go to Jesus for healing, and they are in quite different situations in life, apart from the suffering they are both experiencing (which is different, but suffering often pulls people together).

The leader of the synagogue would have been someone who had the respect of his community, a role model for others, a person with power and prestige because his reputation came from his religious faith, not any kind of secular power. He has a family, as is evidenced by his daughter, and he seems to care for her. The woman who has been hemorrhaging for twelve years is at the other end of the social spectrum. She's a woman, first, which already takes her down in the Jewish hierarchy, but she is also a woman who has been bleeding for twelve years, which also makes her unclean (most scholars see her ailment as something to do with menstrual blood, given the vagueness of the description; if so, there were clear rules that would forbid her from mingling with others). She has spent all of her money trying to find doctors to heal her, so now she is also poor. Given the fact that she spent her money and there's no husband mentioned, we can also assume she's unmarried and probably infertile in a time when women's primary role was reproduction. She is about as low as one can go in her society without being a leper.

Jesus draws such people to him—rich and poor, male and female—in the gospels because he creates an atmosphere of unconditional acceptance. Whether someone is a leader of a synagogue or a poor, unmarried, unclean woman, they are willing to seek Jesus out because of the stories they have heard about him. These stories are so unremarkable because Jesus's life was so remarkable. His consistent acceptance of all who came to him created an environment where everyone felt welcome. There's a reason people invited him to their homes for meals and that a woman washed his feet with her tears and hair.

What matters in this story, then, is not that Jesus heals the girl and woman in this story, but that the leader of the synagogue and the woman crossed societal and religious boundaries to get to Jesus, that Jesus creates a world where such boundaries break down and give people the boldness and freedom to do so. The leader of the synagogue went against the other religious leaders who were trying to catch Jesus in a trap, so they could get rid of him. He believed that Jesus would accept him, despite his position in society, and Jesus did. The woman who was bleeding went into a society that said she should stay outside, and she touched Jesus's robe; an unmarried, unclean woman touched the robe of a Jewish man in public, breaking numerous religious rules, all because she believed Jesus would not condemn her.

Jesus's radical inclusivity creates a world where people feel free to cross whatever boundaries society has set up; they believe not just that Jesus can heal them or their daughters, but that living like Jesus can heal the world of its divisions. In Lamentations, we read of God's faithfulness, and it would be easy to read that passage as a promise that God will heal us when we physically suffer. But we look around the world, and we know that doesn't always happen. Sometimes, daughters die and diseases lead to more suffering, not a dramatic recovery.

God is faithful, though, in providing the faith we need to live through such situations because Jesus has shown us the way to live. If we are all acting out the love and compassion of Jesus, people can survive when their daughters die or when they struggle with a long-term illness because we will be with them, in Jesus's name. We will not let socioeconomic status keep us apart; we will not let gender or marital status keep us apart; we will not let gender identity or sexual orientation keep us apart; we will not let race or ethnicity keep us apart; we will not even let religion keep us apart. We will come together to help others in the midst of their suffering because Jesus's love creates a world where boundaries no longer matter.

We have hope in the Lord, as Lamentations says, because we have seen such love acted out time and time again, not just in Jesus's life, but in our lives and the lives of those around us. We have experienced people reaching across the divides our society tries to set up, and we have reached across them ourselves. We have felt the love and compassion of others, and they have felt ours. We have experienced the kingdom of God here on Earth in those moments, so now we must go out and create those times for others who are suffering, to show them a world without divisions, without barriers, a world that has only love and acceptance.

Questions for Reflection or Discussion:

Talk about times you and/or your church have crossed societal boundaries to help others.

What are the boundaries you and/or your church still need to cross, and what needs can you meet in doing so?

We Can't Always Get What We Want

Seventh Sunday After Pentecost

Luke 11:1–13
Genesis 18:20–33

M ANY PEOPLE STRUGGLE WITH prayer, not just taking the time to pray, but wondering what the purpose behind it even is. We go through long arguments that usually involve what God knows and what God doesn't; ultimately our debates (even if they're simply in our minds) are about the nature of God. If God knows everything and is in control of everything, then we shouldn't even bother with prayer, as God will do what God will do. If God doesn't know everything and/or isn't in control of everything, then we're not sure what good God can even do if we bother to pray. Given the amount of suffering we see in the world, many of us end up at the second conclusion, questioning the efficacy of prayer and the influence of God altogether.

In the gospel of Luke's version of what we now call the Lord's Prayer, we at least get some guidance about how to pray, and it seems drastically different than the way many of us pray, which might reshape the way we think about prayer. The first aspect most of us notice is just how short it is, much shorter than the version from the gospel of Matthew, and it only involves five ideas: an address to God; asking for the kingdom; basic necessities; forgiveness; and temptation. When most of us pray, we might touch on two of those ideas, at best, but we spend much of our time asking for specific events to occur or not occur, and we are often disappointed when life doesn't play out the way we have prayed for.

The rest of the passage from the gospel of Luke complicates matters even more, as Jesus seems to say that the reason we don't get what we want from prayer is because we aren't persistent enough. If only we were as dogged in prayer as the man is who needs to get some bread for his visiting friend, then we, too, would get from God what we ask for. It sounds like all people need to do is devote much more time to prayer, keep asking God over and over for the same events to occur, and, presto, everything in life will work out the way we want. Anybody who has truly prayed for some event to occur or not occur and seen life work out otherwise will question the truth of such an approach. In fact, one of the worst comments we can make to people in the midst of a tragedy is that they didn't have enough faith or they didn't pray enough.

While the opening of this passage is about prayer, the rest of it really isn't about prayer (despite most Bible's adding headings, such as Perseverance in Prayer). It's not about God as much as it is about us. If it is about God, then there are serious problems with Jesus's consistency, as he seems to begin with the parable that describes God as someone we need to constantly annoy to get God to do what we want, but ends with stating how willing God is to give what we want. Within about a minute and a half of talking, Jesus would be presenting two drastically different images of God.

There is nothing in the story Jesus tells, though, that should make us think the friend who is already in bed is God and that the person knocking on the door is a person in prayer. Instead, we have to look back to the prayer Jesus gives to show us what really matters in the verses that follow. Jesus suggests followers pray for the kingdom to come and that we have daily bread, both of which matter greatly to reading this story, the bread showing up on a literal level, as well as metaphorical.

Jesus's idea of the kingdom is one where everyone is welcome and, not coincidentally, everyone has enough to eat (both as a metaphor for ultimate satisfaction and a literal meaning of people simply not going hungry). Essentially, Jesus is suggesting his disciples pray for justice to come to Earth. He wants true equality that comes from love, which also connects to the idea of forgiveness he asks them to pray for (spending one of the six lines pointing out that we have also forgiven others, as that's how the kingdom should work: we are forgiven, so we forgive).

However, as we know, justice doesn't come by our sitting around and praying for it. We have to be out in society, actively working for justice, for it to become a reality. We have to be like the man knocking on the door, demanding that our friend get up out of bed, disturbing his children, and getting bread for our visitors. We have to knock on society's door, bothering whomever we need to bother, again and again and again, until society wakes up and gets people what they need. Doing so is perseverance in prayer only in that we are working to make our prayers a reality; we are working to have God's kingdom come, to provide daily bread for those who don't have it, to forgive all, as we have been forgiven.

We're supposed to be like Abraham in his conversation with God, consistently pushing to see if we can save cities from themselves. God is willing to hear Abraham and agree with him that it is better to try to redeem a city, save people, than simply destroy them. God wants the good gifts for God's children, as the gospel account says, but people often work against what we actually need. Abraham is persistent, but, even with persistence, sometimes people will choose evil, as Sodom and Gomorrah continually chose to be inhospitable, to be unwelcome to visitors, leading to their destruction.

Jesus tells his followers that if they ask or seek or knock, ultimately they will receive or find or have the door opened. We live in the faith that his statement is true, that, if we persevere, we will ultimately see justice. There is no promise that it will happen soon, even in our lifetime, but we will see glimpses of the kingdom if we are persistent. God wants that justice for God's children—everyone on Earth—but God has given us the task not just of praying for it, but for bringing it into being. It is hard work, and it is easy to get discouraged. Thus, we need to pray for one another and for ourselves, that we will have the strength to continue. And then we need to knock until the door is answered.

Questions for Reflection or Discussion:

What do we typically pray for when alone or publicly in church? What might be some other things we could pray for?

Where are places we could act to help our prayers become realities?

Getting and Spending

Eighth Sunday After Pentecost

Luke 12:13–21
Colossians 3:1–11

T HIS PASSAGE FROM THE gospel of Luke is one of Jesus's clearest passages about money and its effects on us. The person in the crowd has what sounds like a fair request to us today, as he simply wants his brother to split the inheritance with him. Since we're not given any more context, we're not completely sure about why Jesus responds the way he does, but it's clear that Jesus thinks the person (probably a man, as women couldn't inherit property at all) is being unreasonable. More than likely, he is a younger son, and, under Jewish law, he would have inherited little of his father's possessions; thus, he's asking Jesus to circumvent traditional inheritance laws by encouraging his older brother to divide the inheritance.

As we have seen so many times, Jesus is willing to break rules where he believes they are harmful to people rather than helpful, but, here, he upholds the law instead. He perceives the man's motivations to be not any type of equality, which is one way we could read the question, but as a means to try to get more than his fair share. Jesus clearly believes greed is motivating the man, and Jesus talks about money and its effects more than any other subject, save for the kingdom. Thus, Jesus takes the opportunity to warn the man and the crowd about greed.

What bothers Jesus about greed here is not simply the acquisition of goods or money, as we all need to do so to live. Jesus knows the problems that greed creates, that it is not simply a problem in itself, but it leads us to behave in ways that harm relationships. The man asking the question will create strife in the family with his request, and it sounds as if there is already conflict there. His asking the question implies that he has already been arguing with his brother about the inheritance, and he is now raising their concerns in a public forum, which will only lead to more problems in the family.

In the parable, it's not relationships that cause the problem because the rich man doesn't seem to have any relationships. There is no mention of a family either when he talks about enjoying what he has stored up or when Jesus talks about what will happen after his death, as it seems no one will inherit what he has been able to accumulate. The implication is that the rich man has focused his life on acquiring property and possessions, and, thus, he has ignored cultivating relationships, which should be what sustains him during his final years.

Talking about greed—or even money, in general—makes us uncomfortable. We tend to avoid it in our churches, save for those times when we have to discuss the church budget and stewardship, though even then we try to broaden out to talk about how we can all contribute in so many ways, including our time and talents, simply implying that giving money is one way we can help the church. One of the most offensive questions we could ask one another today is how much money we make, as it would cross a social taboo that is more entrenched than almost any other.

One of the main problems with talking about money in the contemporary Western world is that our entire society is based around an economic philosophy that encourages us to compete with one another, to defeat one another, in some sense. We talk about capitalism, as if this idea is perfectly normal. Whenever we discuss the economy, we explain how we need more competition to lower prices, as if competition doesn't imply that someone must lose and that loss involves losing a business or a job or a livelihood. We hear about job cuts from major corporations on such a regular basis that we forget that every one of those numbers is a person who will now struggle in ways many of us cannot imagine (unless we are one of those numbers). Capitalism inherently dehumanizes people, as we care more about profits than we do people.

The church's job, then, is to find ways to be counter-cultural when it comes to economics, just as we try to do with so many other ways of thinking. In Colossians, Paul lists greed as a moral issue along with fornication, impurity, passion, and evil desire, all actions that can divide people and communities, as he understands that greed often leads to division, not the unity we're supposed to find in the church. This passage is all about ways we find to divide ourselves, and socioeconomic status is simply one more way we do.

Thus, the church must be willing to talk about money, not in a way that encourages guilt, but in a way that promotes unity. We have to find ways to cooperate, not compete, with one another, to see our economic actions in ways that create community, not division. Rather than shopping at the big box store on the edge of town that doesn't provide benefits to its employees, we can pay more to shop at the smaller, locally-owned stores that treat workers well and contribute to the community in positive ways. However, we can also not shame or create guilt in those members of our churches who cannot afford to pay more, who are barely able to pay those bills, and so they shop at places that are cheaper.

We all must continue to work for a world where all businesses treat their workers fairly, even when it does cost us more, but we also have to work for a world where everyone makes enough money to afford to shop at those places. Those of us with more money can use that money to influence decisions about how society operates; we can make our voices heard with how we spend our money. We can refuse to participate in an economic system that treats people as replaceable parts by buying less, buying only what we truly need, our daily bread, as Jesus calls it.

By doing so, we strive for what Paul does at the end of the passage from Colossians, with communities where there are no longer any divisions, whether because of race or ethnicity or status of freedom, in Paul's list here, or because of gender, sexual orientation, ability, gender identity, age, or socioeconomic class. We can treat one another as people, not worrying about how much money we make, save for when we can help each other financially. We can spend our time with each other, building true community based on true equality in Christ, not building bigger barns for all we have accumulated. Then we will have the community Jesus sought to create.

Questions for Reflection or Discussion:

How has the church traditionally talked about money? And how might we do so differently?

What changes could we make in how we use our money to lead to more socioeconomic equality? What do we have to let go of to allow others to have their daily bread, and are we willing to do so?

Feeding the Hungry
Ninth Sunday After Pentecost

Mark 6:30–44 (see also Matthew 14:13–21)

T HE FEEDING OF THE five thousand (more, of course, as both Matthew and Mark make it clear that that number only includes men, a rare admission of bias) is one of the most well-known stories in the gospels. Many people outside the church know of it, even enough, at times, to reference the loaves and fishes, though they might not know exactly what that phrase refers to. For those who did grow up in the church, this story is a well-worn example of the miraculous powers of Jesus, one more piece of evidence that he's the Messiah.

Even scholars who are skeptical of many of the biblical miracles credit this one as having some sort of historical truth underneath it, especially as the authors of Matthew and Mark repeat the story in the feeding of the four thousand, an odd repetition, given that its only purpose seems to be reiterating the fact that Jesus has the ability to multiply food more than once. More than one story might convince some people, but most people either believe the story about the feeding of the five thousand or they don't; one more story, with a thousand fewer men, isn't going to be more convincing.

What we often overlook in this story, though, is that Jesus does everything he can to avoid performing this miracle. First, the disciples are the ones who notice that the people are hungry, possibly because they are hungry themselves. The passage from the gospel of Mark makes it clear that they didn't have time to eat, so they must have been at least as hungry as the crowd who was following Jesus. We might give the disciples credit here for thinking of others, but it seems they're just as likely to have been thinking about themselves.

Rather than simply accede to their request, Jesus suggests the disciples find a way to feed all of the people, an undertaking that would cost roughly two-thirds of what the average worker would make in a year. Perhaps Jesus is goading the disciples a bit here, knowing that they are hungry themselves; perhaps he wants to get them to think about others in a tangible way rather than use the people's hunger as an excuse to satisfy themselves.

Regardless of why he originally pushes the responsibility back on the disciples, he does so. He wants them to understand that, while he might be able to provide for people's needs, he wants them to do the work themselves. He wants the disciples to do the work of feeding others and feeding themselves rather than relying on him to do so. They've seen him do other miracles, so it would be easy for them to assume he would be willing to do so whenever they needed him to help them out.

Even though scholars grant that something historical happened that led to this story, many are skeptical that Jesus actually fed somewhere around ten thousand people by multiplying bread and fish. What literally happened is less important, though, than why this story matters; we often get caught trying to establish the factuality of miracles, as if we are like the Jews who were always looking for a sign, rather than trying to understand what the gospel writers wanted us to understand about Jesus and how to live as he did.

There are two important ideas about Jesus and Christianity we can take away from this account. First, that shifting of responsibility from Jesus to the disciples is one that mirrors what Jesus calls us to do every day. Too often, we spend our time reading or talking about ways we can work to satisfy the needs of the world—whether that's physical needs, such as hunger, or spiritual needs, such as love and acceptance—rather than simply doing what needs to be done to meet those needs. Like the disciples, we want to come to Jesus with a request and have it answered without our having to do anything.

Faith doesn't work that way, though. Instead, we come to Jesus with all of our failings, and Jesus assures us that we have what we need to do the work he has called us to do. A few loaves and fish might not sound like it's enough to feed a horde of people, but, if we work with the community of believers, united by Jesus's love, then we can do more than we originally imagined. We can take the little we see around us—physical resources, mental capabilities, belief—and Jesus can transform them into much greater than the sum of their parts, as he brings us together for one purpose: providing for people's needs in the name of Jesus.

Second, what's important in this story is not the multiplying of the food, but the fact that Jesus understands that people have physical needs that need to be met. We often think of those needs in tangible terms, such as housing or clothes or food, all of which are necessary, but people often need something equally as important, but that costs us nothing in terms of money: recognition. In Margaret George's novel *Mary Called Magdalene*, Jesus doesn't actually multiply the loaves and fishes, but tells the disciples to give the people whatever they have. When the disciples are surprised by how satisfied the people are with the very little they have received, Jesus tells them, "The offering of the food means more than the food itself. . . . People are dying for lack of interest, and the spirit is hungrier than the body. A word can mean more than a loaf of bread."

We might not have the resources to end poverty in our area or provide shelter for everyone who needs it (though we should certainly work for those goals), but we can provide interest in people as people. We can treat everyone we encounter as human, listening to their fears and hopes, the stories of their lives. We can welcome them into our lives as they welcome us into theirs, sharing our stories, as well. We can give them the word we have, try to feed their spirits as well as their bodies. When we do so, as the gospel of Mark tells us, all will eat and be filled, no matter how much or little food we have for them.

Questions for Reflection or Discussion:

Where are areas where we look to other people or to God to solve problems rather than doing the work ourselves?

Where can the church—locally or globally—help meet the wide variety of people's needs?

Not the Warm and Fuzzy Jesus

Tenth Sunday After Pentecost

Luke 12:49–53
Romans 12:9–21

P EOPLE OFTEN TRY TO contrast the God of the Old Testament and Jesus in the New Testament, portraying God as vengeful and judgmental, while Jesus is loving and accepting of all. While this comparison often holds up, it ignores passages where Jesus sounds much more like the God of the Old Testament (as if the God of the Old Testament had no mercy or love) than how we typically think of Jesus. It suits our purposes to overlook texts like this one from Luke where Jesus is clearly laying out the effects his teachings will actually have.

Given when the author of Luke is writing his gospel (probably around 70 to 90 CE), this passage makes a good deal of sense. Christianity began spreading among the Jewish community, but then quickly expanded into the Gentile world. Not surprisingly, both of those developments caused a significant amount of conflict. Within the Jewish Christian households, families were divided, as many members of those families remained Jewish and didn't convert to Christianity. As Christianity grew in numbers and in strength, many Jews turned against their family members, and there was a great deal of division.

Similarly, there was division between the Jewish Christians and Gentile Christians, seen most clearly in the debate over following Jewish laws, such as circumcision. Jewish Christians believed that Gentiles must essentially become Jews before becoming Christians. Also, many Gentiles had their own religious beliefs, and Christianity's rise caused division in families, just as it did in the Jewish community.

Jesus's teaching, then, clearly connects with this historical background, as families were dividing wherever Christianity spread. He makes it clear that, rather than being widely accepted, people's conversions to Christianity would cause vast rifts in families rather than bringing the peace he has talked about in other places. Jesus doesn't seem happy about these divisions, but he wants people to understand what it means to follow him. Rather than a life of ease, following Jesus leads to more struggle.

We don't talk much about these types of divisions in contemporary America, mainly because they happen so infrequently (though they do still happen). Given America's approach to freedom of religion and the pervasive nature of Christianity (on a surface level), most people are at least accepting of Christians' religious beliefs. If someone comes home and announces that he or she has converted to Christianity, there might be some consternation and frustration, but there would rarely be the kind of division Jesus is talking about here.

Part of the reason that never happens has to do with American Christianity. In the first century, such a change in religion would have been dramatic, leading to a visible change in lifestyle. The person might stop paying any kind of homage to Caesar or to household gods or eating meat sacrificed to idols, as Paul talks about. In the twenty-first century, most of us would hardly notice if someone converted to Christianity, save for the fact that their Sunday mornings would look rather different.

There are few people who convert to Christianity and look to follow the more radical suggestions Jesus makes. They wouldn't get rid of their possessions, for example, nor would we even expect their buying patterns to change. We wouldn't hear them condemning greed or sexism or racism any more than they had previously done in the past. They would be no more or less inclusive than they had been the year before they converted, or at least we wouldn't expect them to. Assuming they were what we would call generally good people before their conversion, we wouldn't anticipate any major differences afterwards.

The passage from Romans, though, presents exhortations to the church in Rome to live a life that was rather different than everyone around them at that time and is significantly different from what we see in our society today. Romans were known for their enjoyment of violent entertainment, such as the gladiator matches, which defined people in terms of their cold-heartedness. Both the people who participated and those who watched wanted to see people die. They took the same approach to war, wanting to crush their enemies and extend their empire as far as they could.

Thus, Paul's encouragement to feed enemies, to extend hospitality to strangers, and to overcome evil with good would have stood in clear contrast to the prevailing culture at the time. It would do the same in our culture today. We live in a time where America has been at war for more than a decade, yet the Christian community has largely been silent on calling for an end to such bloodshed. Even where we think that war might be justified, we have not cried out against the death of civilians, as the number of those casualties climb higher and higher. Instead, we tend to argue that the evil others do should be repaid with evil.

Similarly, as more and more examples of police brutality against minorities come out, the church has not been in the forefront of the protests. Instead, football teams and university professors and people in the streets of cities have taken up the call for such awful acts to stop. While there are always a few churches and leaders that speak out, most of our churches— especially the white ones—have tried to change the Black Lives Matter mantra into All Lives Matter, forgetting the history of oppression that our churches were (and are) often a part of.

While churches, especially mainline denominations, have long accepted women in leadership, outside of that one area, we have largely been silent on the radical inclusion Jesus preached. Christians are not leading the demands for equal pay for equal work or paid parental leave for both genders or an end to the microaggressions women face every day of their lives.

The same could be said for LGBTQ issues. Some denominations and churches have begun allowing same-sex marriages or the ordination of gay and lesbian ministers (note no one seems to be talking about transgender issues with ordination), but we still need lists of churches that are open and affirming, even within denominations that supposedly are welcoming, to make sure LGBTQ Christians have a place to worship.

Such issues will cause division, but Jesus predicted that would happen. We should not shy away from the radical nature of Jesus's teaching simply because one of our members—family or church—will disagree. Instead, we should love one another, as Paul reminds us, but we should also not "lag in zeal," as he also says, whether or not it leads to the type of division Jesus was talking about.

Questions for Reflection or Discussion:

How did you or people around you change when you or they became Christians? What are visible signs in your life that you follow Jesus? Is there a difference between those who grew up in church and those who didn't?

What are issues in contemporary society the church should be more active in that we often ignore?

Surely He Knows Better

Eleventh Sunday After Pentecost

Matthew 15:21–28
Isaiah 56:1, 6–8

T HE PASSAGE FROM ISAIAH clearly reminds us that, even in the Old
Testament, God was reaching out beyond the boundaries of Israel.
The idea that dominates many of our theological discussions is that the
Old Testament is where God chose the nation of Israel to be the people of
God; then, after Jesus, Paul expanded the idea of who could follow God to
include the Gentiles. Here in Isaiah, though, God clearly calls the "foreign-
ers" who love the Lord and keep the covenant, even going so far to declare
that God's house will be "a house of prayer for all peoples," a passage Jesus
quotes when he is overturning tables in the temple.

Jesus clearly knows this approach to be true. Not only does he quote
this passage, but he often quotes Old Testament passages similar to this one,
passages that break down the barriers between Jews and Gentiles. He acts
them out, as well, talking to Samaritans, healing Romans, loving everyone
he comes in contact with. This image of Jesus is largely at the core of how
we think about him and his ministry, especially as progressive Christians.
While everyone else is talking about who's not in, Jesus finds ways to subvert everyone's markers of exclusion. Such radical inclusion is why many of
us are drawn to Christianity in the first place.

And then we get this story from the gospel of Matthew about the Ca-
naanite woman (a Syro-Phoenician woman when she's mentioned in the gospel of Mark), where Jesus not only doesn't want to heal the woman's daughter,
he first doesn't want to speak to her, then he insults her. He moves from giving her no reaction at all to calling her a dog, a clear insult then, as well as

now. And the reason he gives for not healing her daughter is that he was sent only to the Jews, a comment we know isn't true from other gospel stories.

Christians have long struggled with this story, and they've come up with several ways of thinking through it. The most prominent response for years was that Jesus was simply testing the woman's faith. Given how he interacted with every other Gentile he came into contact with (not to mention every other person), this response is so out of character for Jesus that he definitely had a hidden motive. Once the woman responds with the appropriate faith, he quickly praises her and promises her that her daughter will be healed, and she is, at that very moment.

Those scholars who look at the authorship and readership of the gospels often remind us that the gospel of Matthew was more than likely written from a Jewish author to a Jewish audience. Thus, they conclude, the author of Matthew is centering Jesus in the Jewish tradition, focusing only on Jesus's mission to Israel, as he is King of the Jews, not of anyone else. They point out that most of the stories about Gentiles are in the gospels of Luke or John, gospels that are much more focused on Jesus's ministry to those who weren't Jews.

Last, there are people who argue that this story shows Jesus's humanity. While Jesus had some sort of connection to the divine, they say, he was very much a person. As such, he struggled as we all do, and he had his bad days as well as his good days. This event happened on one of his bad days where he was frustrated and tired, and he ended up taking it out on this innocent woman who simply wanted her daughter healed. The inclusion of this story, then, serves to show us a humanized Jesus who can understand our struggles because he had them, as well.

For most of us, none of these explanations help us understand this story on any significant level. If Jesus is testing the woman to make sure she has enough faith, then he is simply being cruel, as the woman has come because she loves her daughter and wants Jesus to heal her. Turning that situation into a test—and insulting her in the process—doesn't show the love and compassion Jesus acts out in every other situation; it shows someone who is capricious and hurtful, not a person who would have drawn others to him.

If the author of Matthew was angling his story to his readership in such a way to make Jesus out to be hurtful, then he wasn't a strong author, as even Jewish readers would have found such a portrayal off-putting. If Jesus could behave this way to her, there would be nothing to keep him from acting that way toward them. Similarly, though most of us want to see

Jesus's struggles, portraying him as the equivalent of one of us, someone who insults a person who doesn't deserve it, is not a way to get us to model our lives after him. No, none of these explanations help us.

And that's where we're left with this story: without explanations. We don't have any good way to explain why Jesus behaves the way he does, and we simply have to live in that place where our rational answers don't satisfy us. There are, unfortunately, many areas in a life of faith where we do so (the nature of evil, whether or not we have free will, for example), where we can have an answer that satisfies us on a rational or emotional level, but not both. In the letters he wrote to a young poet, Rainer Maria Rilke writes, "You are so young, so much before all beginning, and I would like to beg you, dear Sir, as well as I can, to have patience with everything unresolved in your heart and to try to love the questions themselves as if they were locked rooms or books written in a very foreign language. Don't search for the answers, which could not be given to you now, because you would not be able to live them. And the point is, to live everything. Live the questions now. Perhaps then, someday far in the future, you will gradually, without even noticing it, live your way into the answer."

Unfortunately, we have to make peace with our lack of understanding, not in a way that excuses what we don't understand (none of us would condone Jesus's behavior here), but in a way that acknowledges there is mystery in the universe. If we are patient with life and faith, we can often live our way into the answers, or at least live our way into accepting the lack of answers. But sometimes we won't be able to, and we have to learn to at least accept that reality. We want answers, but sometimes all we're left with are questions.

Questions for Reflection or Discussion:

How have you heard this story interpreted? What interpretation makes the most sense to you?

Where are places in your faith where you have to live without answers, where you have to live the questions, as Rilke says?

Who Do We Say He Is?

Twelfth Sunday After Pentecost

Matthew 16:13–20

T HE EARLY CHURCH SPENT their first few hundred years, give or take, trying to decide what they believed about Jesus. It's one of the reasons we have the Apostles' Creed and, especially, the Nicene Creed, which spends much more time laying out who Jesus is. That debate also shaped the gospels and shaped the canon, guiding which gospel accounts became official church documents and which ones did not. We can even see the evolution of how the church thought about Jesus in the gospels themselves. Mark, the earliest of the four, has no account of Jesus's birth and childhood, and the portrayal of the resurrection is thin, at best. By Matthew and Luke, though, we have fuller accounts of the resurrection and clear stories about Jesus's birth. John skips Jesus's birth—but only to put him as existing since the beginning of time—and provides the most detailed account of the resurrection and post-resurrection Jesus. The emphasis moves from a Jesus who is more of a man to a Jesus who is very much divine.

That divide is one that continues to plague the church, as contemporary followers of Jesus, especially on the progressive side of the faith, struggle with how to talk about Jesus. Traditionally, the church talked about Jesus as being equally human and divine, but not in a 50–50 split fashion. Instead, Jesus was somehow one hundred percent human and one hundred percent divine, a concept, much like the trinity, that humans struggle to understand or explain to others. Because the Bible portrays Jesus as both, he must be both, but he must be equally both, or something is lost, so the traditional interpretation goes.

And then there's the idea of the Messiah or the Christ, in Greek. Peter proclaims Jesus to be the Messiah, and Jesus praises him for it, but then turns around and tells the disciples not to tell anyone that he is so. The idea of the Messiah has political and theological consequences, as the Jews were waiting for a Messiah who would reinstate the reign of David, overthrowing the Romans, and instituting a new theocracy for Israel. Jesus seems to take on this mantle, yet clearly subverts it, proclaiming a gospel of love and forgiveness, not a new political approach to the problems of his followers.

On top of Peter's calling Jesus the Messiah, he also refers to him as the Son of God. There are Old Testament passages that refer to all people as sons or daughters of God, but Peter goes beyond that here, connecting the idea of the Messiah to the idea of the Son of God. In some way, then, Peter sets Jesus apart from the rest of us. The church has typically interpreted this designation to mean that Jesus is, in fact God (as the Nicene Creed says, "God of God, Light of Light, very God of very God; begotten, not made, being of one substance with the Father, by whom all things were made").

In the twenty-first century, though, people struggle both with the idea of Jesus as Messiah and as Son of God, as the church has typically interpreted both of those terms. People point out the historical development of the gospels and argue that Jesus probably didn't have some sort of divine birth, that the gospel writers added those narratives later to establish Jesus as divine. They make similar arguments about the resurrection or at least call its historicity into question. The past hundred years of historical research into the gospels cause us to question both of these claims, running the risk of turning Jesus into *just* another prophet or person.

It's that *just* that often causes the problem here. People tend to take an either-or approach to thinking about Jesus, arguing that he is either the Messiah, the Son of God ("very God of very God," again) or he is just like any of us or maybe like some of the Old Testament prophets, at best. Then, if people can't accept that idea of Jesus as divine, they tend to leave the faith altogether, arguing that such beliefs are outdated, rooted in a pre-scientific and pre-historical world that centered lives in myths, not what we would call reality.

There are other ways of thinking about Jesus, though, that combine these two approaches, giving us ways of seeing Jesus as someone who should guide us, taking the best of both of these ideas to portray a Jesus even a twenty-first century believer can accept. I will readily admit that there are those Christians who would argue that I am watering down the core of Christianity, that if one cannot admit, as Peter does, that Jesus is the

Messiah, the Son of God, then she or he cannot be a Christian. They would point to verses in Acts that call on people to believe such a dogma. However, throughout the gospels, Jesus undercuts any attempt to define what people must or must not believe in order to obtain any type of salvation, however one defines that term, whether that's Nicodemus coming to him at night or the thief on the cross who espouses no theology at all, yet will join Jesus in paradise, he says.

As such, what Jesus's life, ministry, and death should show us is how to be in this world. Rather than viewing Jesus's existence as some sort of theological proof for his role as the Messiah, the Son of God, we should view Jesus as someone who was more connected to God than any of the rest of us have ever been able to reach. Whether because Jesus was, in fact, "very God of very God" or because God chose him to live out the gospel in a way that others would want to model their lives on him or because he somehow found a connection to the divine that exceeds most mortals, what matters is what Jesus did and what Jesus calls us to do.

There is no *just* when talking about Jesus because he lived a life that exemplified God's love and grace in ways no one else has. He saw the limitations his society placed on him and others, and he crossed them, time and time again, loving those on the margins, touching those who were untouchable. He walked into Jerusalem, the seat of power, and spoke truth to that power, knowing full well what the consequences of those actions would be, seeking justice for everyone, dying for that belief. Jesus is not *just* anything; Jesus is everything God has called us to be, no matter what term we use to describe him.

Questions for Reflection or Discussion:

How do you think about Jesus as Son of God or Messiah? What do those terms mean to the church today?

When you think about Jesus as *human* or *divine*, what do those terms mean for the way you view him?

What to Worship

Thirteenth Sunday After Pentecost

Luke 14:25–35
Deuteronomy 30:15–20

P EOPLE HAVE MISUSED THE passage from the gospel of Luke time and
time again over the years, demanding people shift their allegiance from
their family to the church (or the leaders of the church). Often, church
leaders have used this passage to control people, especially women, trying
to separate them from those who care about them in order to manipulate
them. Rather than using this passage to encourage people to look to God,
leaders have used it to have people look to them, drawing on the idea of
carrying the cross to explain away any suffering that happens along the way.

What those leaders have often ignored is a verse that comes near the
end of this section of the gospel of Luke, where Jesus, out of nowhere, tells
his listeners that people cannot be his disciples if they do not give up all of
their possessions. That one verse comes after Jesus's explanation of the cost
of discipleship, but it just doesn't seem to fit here, as if it's a thought that Jesus almost forget to mention, but snuck in just before moving on to talking
about salt. My guess is that the leaders who use this section to manipulate
others certainly don't follow that verse in any literal way, but they might
encourage their followers to do something along those lines.

Reading this passage in its entirety is important to understanding what
Jesus is really talking about here. We know he's not talking about hating our
parents or family members, and he's not even arguing that we give up all of our
possessions (there are a group of women the author of Luke mentions who
financially support Jesus's ministry; there's no way they could have done so if
they gave up all of their possessions). Instead, Jesus is talking about priorities

and how they have a tendency to get skewed by a culture that doesn't value what God does and that does value the shallow and superficial.

Jesus wants to remind us that our society (as his did) focuses on status and wealth and possessions as a measure of who was important and who wasn't. Society argues that we should work as much as we can to make as much money as we can, so we can live a life that satisfies us, so people will revere us because of that success. Such an approach says that people who do work that doesn't lead to a high salary—teaching or social work or refugee resettlement, for example—aren't successful people. Such an approach says that people who live on the streets aren't as valuable as those who live in nice houses. Such an approach says that people who aren't the right gender or race or ethnicity or sexual orientation or gender identity or ability do not deserve the same respect as those of us who are. Society judges by appearances, not by the grace and love of God, who sees all as worthy of love and respect.

The passage from Deuteronomy sets out the choice quite clearly: we can choose to bow down to other gods (wealth, socioeconomic status, possessions, attributes) that society gives us and we can perish, or we can choose to love God and live. Worshiping the gods that society presents leads to death because we will be empty inside, focusing only on our happiness or how society perceives us, always worried that we're not living up to the status quo, leaving us hollow and without life. Loving God, though, leads to our loving our neighbors as ourselves, creating a world where we value everyone, no matter what they own or don't or what they look like or what kind of job they have, if any. Loving God leads to a life full of community and support because others return that love when they experience it, creating the kingdom here on Earth.

The part of the passage from Luke that is confusing, though, is when Jesus talks about counting the cost of discipleship. He uses the metaphors of people building a tower or waging a war, pointing out that no one would do either of those without planning ahead of time; otherwise, they would end up looking foolish or losing a war. The implication here is that those who were listening should think seriously about following Jesus, that they should weigh the costs of doing so before following him. For those early followers and the early church, those costs were severe, as they might, in fact, lose their families or their lives.

However, none of us can truly weigh the costs of living a life where Jesus leads, as we cannot truly understand what those costs might look like. There are people, even today, who lose their families because of their faith when they didn't expect to do so. People agree to take on the powerful because of their faith, and they end up losing their lives in the process. They have gone to protest wars in foreign countries or take their skills to places where the need is greatest or bear witness to the suffering in places, and they have died in the process. Even in smaller ways, when people work for less because they believe they can share the love of God to those whom society deems unlovable, and they give up good healthcare or retirement to do so, they give up part of their lives.

There is no way any of us can truly count that cost at the outset, that we can know what will wait for us when we make those choices. Society, in fact, believes we are like the man building the tower only to find that he does not have enough to finish it, and they see him as a fool. Because we value what others don't, society looks askance at us. However, when we make these choices, when we choose what God values over what the world values, when we put aside what the world worships, we find a life we couldn't have imagined otherwise.

The costs exist, as we see again and again, and we would be foolish not to try to consider them. However, we cannot let what society thinks shape how we behave. Instead, we must try to find a way to hear God in the midst of the noise of the world, to hear from those around us whom the Spirit speaks through, and get rid of what the world wants us to own, to live how God wants us to live. Only by doing so will we have true life rather than living as if we were dead, no matter how long we live.

Questions for Reflection or Discussion:

What are things or people or ideas society tells us to value that prevent our seeing God?

What are some of the costs of following Jesus that we often overlook or forget about?

What We've Lost

Fourteenth Sunday After Pentecost

Luke 15:1–10
Ezekiel 34:11–24

P EOPLE OFTEN OVERLOOK THESE two parables from the gospel of Luke or only include them when they're talking about the one that comes after them, the one we refer to as the parable of the Prodigal Son, combining all of the parables about something or some person that gets lost in some way. Even then, the focus tends to be on the more famous of the three parables. Part of that emphasis is because we're more interested in a story about a son and a father and their relationship than we are on a woman who loses a coin or even a shepherd who loses a sheep. Jesus seems more interested in the last parable, as well, as he gives much more detail in its telling than he does with the first two, the second of which is only three sentences.

However, these two parables have something to say about the nature of God, humanity, and the kingdom, as well, so they're worth our time. The parable of the lost sheep resonates more than the one about the lost coin for the same reason we focus on the parable of the Prodigal Son: we care more about a sheep than we do a coin. However, the coin seems to be more valuable to the woman than the sheep to the shepherd on a practical level. The coin is worth roughly a day's wages, which isn't much overall. For example, if one makes $50,000 a year today, the coin would be worth just under $140; we would be upset if we lost $140, but not if we make $50,000 a year. The woman, though, only has ten of the coins, which makes them more valuable to her.

The sheep, though, is one of a hundred, and it is more easily replaceable. Sheep reproduce and have other sheep, while the coins don't replace themselves nearly as easily. One could invest to try to earn interest, but that's the only option for reproducing coins. Sheep, though, are alive, and we care more about living beings than we do mere money. Or at least we say we do. If we need that money to live, we might want the money more than we want the sheep, and this woman definitely needs money. Given that there's no mention of her having a family in this parable (she celebrates with friends and neighbors), she's either an unmarried woman or a widow, so she has no male to support her, which she would have needed in Israel. Thus, this coin is important to her in a way a sheep wouldn't be.

In both cases, though, it's the person who possesses the sheep and the coin that give them value. We might not value a sheep at all, but the shepherd cares enough about that sheep to leave the ninety-nine vulnerable in the wilderness while he goes to find that sheep. The woman is willing to disrupt her household at night to find that coin, a coin we might ignore, chalking up the loss or at least waiting until it's light outside.

Jesus's point here, then, comes from the context of the parables, a context we often ignore when talking about these parables, especially if we skip these two. Tax collectors and sinners (it's odd how vague this term is, as the sinners must have been clearly recognizable, but we're not told what they're particular sin is) come to listen to Jesus, which leads the Pharisees and scribes to grumble about who Jesus associates with. As he often does, rather than arguing theology with the religious leaders, he tells them stories designed to illustrate how Jesus believes the world should be.

In this case, he sums up his view at the end of each parable, pointing out that God rejoices when even one person who has not been a part of the kingdom becomes a part. It is God that gives each of us value because God already loves and cares for us, whether we are tax collectors or sinners or religious leaders or disciples. God created us with value because God created us with love; it is only humanity that takes away any value by treating each other as less than human.

In Ezekiel, the author sets up this dichotomy clearly. The first half of the passage focuses on God as a shepherd who cares for the flock. As in the parables, God here will look for those who have strayed away, caring for those who are injured, and giving strength to those who are weak. God will even feed the sheep with justice. This passage sounds like a description of the kingdom. From then on, though, the author talks about how some sheep want more than others and, in so doing, ruin the paradise God has given the sheep. The powerful have pushed the weak aside, wanting more than their share, scattering the animals yet again.

God, though, steps in again, pointing out how God shall give them a shepherd, as they clearly cannot take care of themselves. Even when God has given them justice, they revert to the systems they have known that favor the strong and oppress the weak. The author of Ezekiel is clearly referring to how Israel has behaved over the course of its history, how they came out of Egypt into a land flowing with milk and honey, but then how they took that paradise and turned it into another type of slavery. Those with power used it to oppress those below them rather than following the law that clearly protects the marginal.

God will seek out the lost sheep and feed us with justice. However, that justice only comes through the hands and feet of God, through those of us who are part of the flock opening up our communities to other people, those tax collectors and sinners whom the religious leaders would keep out. As long as we say that people of different races or ethnicities, those who are LGBTQ, people who are differently abled are not welcome, we will pollute the paradise God has given us. God has fed us justice, but we must then take what we have been given and share it with others. Those of us who are stronger, by whatever power or status we have in our society, must give what we have away, making ourselves less so that others can be more. When we are able to do so, we will feed others with justice, and there will be much rejoicing in heaven.

Questions for Reflection or Discussion:

Who are people society does not give value to, but whom the church could and should?

What are some ways those who have more (whether money or privilege or anything else) could give some away so that others might have enough?

Ending the Cycle

Fifteenth Sunday After Pentecost

Matthew 18:21–35
Genesis 50:15–21

T HERE HAVE BEEN TIMES in my life when I have been more cynical
about faith than I am now, and one of the ways that cynicism affected
my view of the world was in the difference (or lack thereof) between those
of us who professed to be Christians and those who didn't. I used to say that
the only difference between Christians and non-Christians was whose car
was in the driveway on Sunday mornings. Since I spent most of my life in
the South, I lived in a world where Christian values permeated the culture,
even for those who didn't attend church, so I was missing at least one major
distinction. I didn't see it until I moved to the Pacific Northwest, and I met
a number of people who, as kind as they were, didn't forgive others.

We often sing "They'll Know We Are Christians By Our Love," but
I wonder if we shouldn't add a verse to that or create a new song about
how people would know we are Christians because of our willingness to
forgive. People can often be kind or polite to others, pretending even to love
them, but forgiveness seems a much harder task. And I know that people
can't really love each other unless they have forgiven whoever has wronged
them, but we seem more willing to pretend to love than we are to pretend
to forgive. Forgiveness seems more personal in some way.

This passage from the gospel of Matthew also shows us how much of
a challenge it is, as the servant in the parable receives an amazingly generous offer of forgiveness, an exaggerated portrayal, in fact, as it would have
been almost impossible for him to become as indebted as he was. He takes
that forgiveness, then proceeds not to grant a much lesser version of that

forgiveness to a fellow servant. This parable seems easy to interpret: God has forgiven us of so much, we should then forgive everyone of whatever they do, as it cannot measure up to the forgiveness God and others have given us. If we don't forgive others, God will cast us into hell where we will be tortured for all eternity.

That's traditionally how we have interpreted this parable, and the first section of it works well. God has forgiven us and continues to forgive us; other people have also forgiven us, so we should forgive others. However, the part about God's casting us into hell for that lack of forgiveness seems out of place here. The passage is all about how forgiving God is, but then God ceases to be forgiving and switches to condemning us for our lack of forgiveness, which seems rather ironic. Some Christians would argue that God's forgiveness has limits, whether of how much we can do wrong before we cross some line (and we argue over what that line is on a regular basis) or the time frame we have, as God's forgiveness stops when we die, then switches to strict judgment.

There is another way to read the ending of this parable, though. Throughout the Old Testament, God talks about visiting the sins of the fathers on the children, sometimes to multiple generations. That sounds terribly unfair, as if God wants to see the innocent suffer for the wrongs of the guilty. A.J. Jacobs, in his book *The Year of Living Biblically*, tells a story that helps us see this idea in a different way, which will help us with the passage from the gospel of Matthew. Jacobs spends a year trying to live out all of the commandments in the Bible literally. At one point, he reads a verse about sins of the fathers being passed on to children, and he has a common experience that helps him understand. Something goes wrong, and he says a word he doesn't want his son to imitate, yet his son does. Jacobs realizes that God is not the one passing the sins on from one generation to another; we are the ones who do so.

No matter how we behave, for good or ill, children will imitate us. Even if we don't have children, if we are ever around them—whether as relatives or as teachers or at church—they will pick up on what we do and try to behave like us. An obvious example of generational sin is abuse, where a parent abuses a child who then grows up to abuse his or her child. Some people break out of such a cycle, but it is challenging to do so. Oppression and injustice become ingrained in our lives.

In the same way, when Jesus uses this language, he is speaking in the same way the authors of the Old Testament did, but it is not God who will punish us by sending us to some sort of eternal torment. Instead, if we live without forgiveness in our lives, we will torment ourselves for as long as we live. If we hold on to grudges or wrongs, we will cease to see the beauty of this world, only looking for more places where others have done us wrong; we will cease to trust others, knowing they will only fail us in the long term. We will lose whatever true contentment we have.

Joseph understood this idea of forgiveness, as his brothers made him suffer greatly, selling him into slavery (after planning to kill him), which led to his being imprisoned for years. They acted out of envy and distrust, which dominated their lives. Joseph, though, knew the only way they could all continue to live as a family was if he forgave them, and he did.

Forgiveness is one of the most important aspects of a life of faith, as people have done great injustice to one another over the centuries. As with Joseph, we built America by enslaving others and using them to bring economic stability to the few. We have a society where women make less money than men, where it is unsafe for them to walk wherever and whenever they want, where they have to endure comments and treatment that men cannot imagine. We live in a world where we design buildings and jobs and homes for people with certain abilities, limiting those with others, keeping them from achieving what they are capable of. We have a world where people of different sexual orientations or gender identities fear for their safety, are unable to take the jobs they would want, or are even unable to buy a wedding cake, depending on where they live. We have a country where we see those who hope to come to America to better their lives as people who will drain our resources and take our jobs rather than improve us all, as immigrants and refugees have done for centuries.

However, God calls us to forgive even these wrongs. That does not mean we should accept them, as we should always work to end these injustices, but we cannot do so by hating others for their sins. We must acknowledge where we play a part in these wrongs and seek to end them, wherever we see them. We must also forgive ourselves and others for what we have done to perpetuate these injustices. Only then can we create a truly just world, a world where love triumphs over evil and reconciliation is possible.

Questions for Reflection or Discussion:

What is it in our lives that makes it difficult to forgive?

What are small or large injustices we see in the world where we need to offer forgiveness, both to ourselves and others?

Radical Grace

Sixteenth Sunday After Pentecost

Matthew 20:1–16
Isaiah 55:6–9

T HIS PARABLE FROM THE gospel of Matthew is the epitome of the radical inclusivity of God's grace. The landowner readily admits that his logic is not the logic of the workers, that he is more generous than some might want him to be. He even goes so far as to accuse those who have worked the entire day that they are simply envious, that they are not seeking fairness as much as they simply want more for themselves.

Of course, if we're honest with ourselves, we often react in just such a way to God's grace. Those of us who do what we are supposed to do—attend church every week, volunteer for committees or any work the church needs done, read our Bibles, pray regularly, practice any kind of spiritual disciplines—are quite envious when it comes to God's grace. We might say we want the kind of extreme acceptance that Jesus talks about in this parable, but, really, we want people to do what we do, essentially to earn their way into God's good graces.

The passage from Isaiah, though, makes it clear that God's ways are not our ways, and God's thoughts are not our thoughts. In fact, God's ways and thoughts are higher than our ways and thoughts. God will "abundantly pardon," the author of Isaiah tells us because God has mercy on us, even when others would say we don't deserve it. Rather than a God who keeps a scoresheet, as we often do, God begins with a clean sheet every time we come to God, giving love and acceptance in measures we cannot begin to imagine.

The focus in the parable, though, is on the payment at the end, as if that is the only place where we see God's grace. However, the hiring process itself reveals a God who is persistent in seeking out those in need of acceptance. The landowner goes to hire workers five different times throughout the day, beginning early in the morning and ending at five o'clock, even though he knows that they will stop working at six o'clock, based on the other workers' complaints that those hired last only worked one hour. The landowner must know that he will not get much work from people who only work one hour, but the work they do is enough for him; he seems satisfied that he was able to give them that work, as if his hiring them was more for them than for him.

In fact, when the landowner asks them why they have done no work that day, they reply that no has hired them. People can easily read this section of the parable as leading to the Puritan work ethic, pointing out that these workers were clearly eager to work, but no one hired them. Some might argue that the landowner (and, thus, God) is only seeking people who are willing to work for their pay, even if they only work an hour.

However, there are other reasons employers don't hire workers, as our contemporary society reminds us. It seems odd that so many workers have stood around all day, yet no one hired them. The landowner, though, finds people looking for work every time he goes back to do so. No one has hired these workers not because they don't need workers, but because they didn't see these workers as valuable for whatever reason. The last-hired workers don't say that no one has come looking for workers; they say that no one has hired them, an important difference.

In the same way that the landowner keeps coming back for those workers whom no one has hired, God consistently reaches out to those people society overlooks, welcoming them and treating them like everyone else. If one wants to view this parable historically, we can easily see the progression of God's connecting to Abraham and Moses and the early Israelites, then spreading that relationship to the Gentiles and on to the wider world, with everyone as equals. In our contemporary society, though the church has been slow to accept God's vision, we are beginning to move that direction. For years, in America, the church at large didn't accept African Americans as equals, then it was women, now it is people who are LGBTQ and those who are differently abled. Though we still need to make much more progress, more and more churches are beginning to see God's vision.

That view of the world is one that says our churches and the kingdom are open to anyone and everyone, no matter what they look like or who they love or what socioeconomic status they are in or what they can or cannot do or how they experience their gender identity. The landowner sees the workers, even those at five o'clock, as people who are equally able to do the work of the kingdom, so he hires them and rewards them accordingly. God sees each of us, every child of God, as worthy of love and grace, no matter what society says about us. God's ways are not our ways, and God's thoughts are not our thoughts, and God's vision of the kingdom is not our vision of the kingdom. Thank God for that.

Questions for Reflection or Discussion:

Where are places in society where we need to see more of God's radical inclusivity?

What are ways we can begin to dispel the idea that others must do as we do in order to be the right kind of Christian?

Doubts and Questions
Seventeenth Sunday After Pentecost

Mark 9:14–29
James 3:1–12

THE VERSE THAT COMES about two-thirds of the way through this passage from the gospel of Mark—"I believe; help my unbelief!—is one of the more famous passages, especially among those of us who grew up in more evangelical churches, only to move to the progressive side of faith as we got older. Growing up in an evangelical setting, church leaders or parents didn't allow us to have any sort of unbelief, as that showed that our faith was weak (or nonexistent). Parents or pastors or friends told us we simply needed to believe more, to pray more, to trust God (or the church leaders or parents) more, and we would be fine.

However, somewhere along the way, our doubts and questions pushed us further and further away, and, at least for some, leaving the church became the only viable alternative. We didn't know there were other ways of being Christian; we had to learn that later, which provided a way back into faith and the church. We learned that we could hold both of these statements to be true at the same time, that, perhaps, they were also true at the same time, no matter what our situation.

That's especially true when we look at the entire passage, this story about a man whose son is possessed by a demon (or at least a spirit) that the disciples cannot cast out. We live in a time and sub-set of Christianity that doesn't grant much validity to demons or spirits that possess other people. We read scholars who find various ways of explaining this story in more believable terms. They talk about how the son was epileptic, but Jesus treated the boy with compassion, treated him as a human being, providing a type of healing that wasn't typical for the society. They provide other interpretations, such as reading the boy as suffering from some rabies-like disease that Jesus, as an itinerant healer, was able to cure in some way, but that became conflated into a miraculous healing.

Modern Christians embrace such readings, as they portray Jesus as someone who loves and cares for those around him, but who doesn't have any supernatural abilities (beyond the ability to love and care for everyone he meets). It's our way of making sense of stories that no longer make sense in a scientific world. We talk about how writers in a less enlightened time describe situations that we can make much more sense out of and how these stories still contain truth for us.

Essentially, we're trying to believe the story, while we don't really believe it. We're trying to find ways that make the Bible more believable, more relevant, while disbelieving the literal events in it. We use the same approach throughout the Old Testament, as we reconcile the creation accounts with evolution or find ways to explain how a partial, tribal, violent God could turn into the loving Jesus who accepts all he encounters, no matter their ethnic or religious background.

This story speaks to us because Jesus doesn't condemn the man for his combination of belief and unbelief; instead, Jesus heals his son and gives him back to his father. We seek out stories like this one or about Thomas's supposed doubting because they validate the struggles we modern Christians have, with our doubts and our disbelief, combined with our urgent desire to believe and have faith. We live in the middle of this tension, and we are unable to find a way out of it, and so validation is all we can find.

The passage from the book of James seems to have nothing to do with this struggle, as the author talks about our speech and our lack of control over it. We say what we know we shouldn't, and we don't say what we know we should. Instead of sharing love with our speech, we make hurtful comments, often to the people we love the most. We see injustice in the world, and we fail to speak out against it, preferring to protect our status over someone else's humanity. We find ourselves in the middle of yet another situation: one of action and inaction as opposed to belief and disbelief.

What these passages both teach us, then, is that this dilemma is the human condition, whether we are on the progressive end of faith or the conservative one or somewhere in between, whether we are on either end of the political spectrum, or wherever else we find ourselves in life. We want to believe in various institutions, whether they are political or spiritual or economic, yet those institutions have let us down so many times, we don't believe any longer, as we don't want to be the fool one more time. We want to believe in people around us, as they have offered love and support before, but they have also hurt us in ways we wonder if we can forgive, so we keep our distance from them. We want to believe in ourselves, that we will do what is right, even when doing so will harm ourselves, but we have let ourselves down so many times, we don't believe we will do so. We live in the middle of action and inaction, belief and disbelief, every day of our lives.

What the passage from the gospel of Mark enables us to see is that, though the disciples let the man down and he doesn't believe as much as he might want to, Jesus does not. Whether Jesus literally casts out a demon or simply shows the boy the love and compassion he deserves, Jesus gives the man and his son what they need in this moment. The man will continue to doubt, and the son will have questions later in his life, but Jesus will still meet them in the middle of those concerns, providing what they need.

We, too, will continue to live in the middle of our struggles, questioning biblical stories, our churches, each other, ourselves, even Jesus. Yet God will not be bothered by those questions, as Jesus walked through this world in the middle of them, meeting people where they were, not where others wanted them to be. He will meet us in the middle of our concerns, showing us the love and compassion others can't always give us. The questions won't go away, but neither will Jesus's attention.

Questions for Reflection or Discussion:

Where are places or issues we live in the midst of belief and unbelief, action and inaction?

What can the church do to help us as we live in those tensions?

Hearing the Margins
Eighteenth Sunday After Pentecost

Matthew 21:33–46
Isaiah 5:1–7

I T'S SO EASY TO attack the religious leaders of Jesus's day; he certainly did. He pointed out their hypocrisies and how they had lost the meaning behind all of the rules and regulations they followed (and, more importantly, imposed on others). He also regularly reminded them that they were not set apart from anyone else simply because they were Jews, which often led to passages like this one from the gospel of Matthew, where he clearly states, at the end of the parable, that he is interested in actions, not heredity.

The religious leaders (like most Jews) were looking for a particular kind of Messiah, one who would restore Israel in a military and political sense, not only a spiritual one. When Jesus didn't fulfill their expectations, they attacked him and tried to trap him with complex theological questions. Jesus didn't hesitate to return those attacks, pointing out everything they had gotten wrong about the religion they were supposedly experts of, reminding them of passages from the Torah they ignored or rationalized to mean what they wanted them to mean. Given our distance from such an environment, it's quite easy then for us to attack them for all they got wrong or didn't see.

This parable is one of Jesus's most direct attacks, coming shortly before they will arrest him and turn him over to the Romans for crucifixion. This passage either leads to that arrest or comes from Jesus's knowledge that his remaining time is short. In the parable, Jesus clearly lays out what the religious establishment has done to the inheritance they had; rather than embrace the prophets and their calls to reform, religious and political leaders throughout Israel's history condemned those prophets, sometimes even putting them to death. Jesus knows that the same fate waits for him, that only the crowds are keeping the religious leaders at bay for a bit longer.

While it's easy to criticize these leaders from our different time and culture, we also have to remember that this parable applies to us as much as to them. We are the religious leaders now, whether we are ministers or elders or simply profess to be Christian at some level. Despite Americans' professions of faith, fewer and fewer people are actively involved in any formal religious practices. Though most Americans say they believe in God, more people profess that they are "spiritual, not religious" than can state what they actually believe in any theological sense. Even within churches in America today, most people talk more about what attendance gives them or helps them feel than what that faith demands of them.

The question, then, becomes what we religious leaders are missing today. In the same way that the Pharisees and chief priests could not see that Jesus was speaking the truth they needed to hear, we are surely not hearing or speaking some truth the world needs today. We're human, just as they were human, so we need to continually remind ourselves that we, too, have our limitations, and we must seek them out in places and from people where we would not expect to find them. As Wendell Berry once wrote, "If change is to come, it will come from the margins . . . It was the desert, not the temple, that gave us the prophets."

The church's history of listening to those on the margins is not strong. We ignored the voices calling for us to stop the practice of slavery, as the church often defended the practice, relegating many people to subhuman status. We refused to hear women and their supporters calling for equality, and we used the Bible to support vile actions, including domestic abuse, against women. We stood on the sidelines of the civil rights movement, watching our brothers and sisters as people attacked and even killed them, even using our pulpits to support segregation. Even now, we refuse to act on behalf of our LGBTQ sisters and brothers who seek equality in the legal and political realm, but also in churches, where they wish to worship. We especially struggle with supporting people with sexual identities some of us don't understand, such as transgender, intersexual, or asexual people, as those of us who are straight, cisgendered individuals struggle to comprehend those differences.

As the passage from Isaiah reminds us, we are a vineyard God has tended with loving care. For those of us with privilege, we know society and culture have given us so much, but, as with Israel's history, we have often squandered that privilege. We have either wallowed in guilt, never moving to action, or used our status to segregate ourselves from those who were different than we are.

Throughout the church's history, we have been two steps behind whatever civil rights changes were going on in America, often admitting decades later where we were wrong and asking for forgiveness. Like those who began following Jesus only after his death and resurrection (Paul, for example), we support people long after their fight has begun, sometimes as it has changed into less visible battles that don't require us to sacrifice our reputations. Rather than leading such movements, reminding the world of the radical inclusivity of God's kingdom, we have ignored the cries of prophets we didn't recognize.

While there is still much work we need to do for true equality in America for those of different races, abilities, sexual orientations, gender identities, genders, ethnicities, we must also work to hear those on the margins who are trying to tell us where we should go in the future. While we work for those who have struggled for decades or centuries, we must also search for those who are just beginning their struggle, so that we might find ways to amplify their voices, to walk with them and support them in whatever way we can. We must be, as Jesus says, "a people that produces the fruits of the kingdom," rather than waiting for decades, only to apologize after others have fought for equality.

It is time for the church to be a shaper of culture, not one more institution that reacts to it long after the serious work of beginning a movement has happened. Jesus reshaped the world through love and compassion and acceptance, and we must do the same, even when—especially when—it is unpopular to do so. We don't know where the next voices will come from, but we must listen to the margins, the desert, then bring those voices into our churches, where we can welcome them and tell them we and God love them.

Questions for Reflection or Discussion:

Where are the voices on the margins we might listen to today? And how can those of us with privilege help amplify those voices?

What social justice issues could the church get involved in now that we have been ignoring? How can those of us with privilege use it for good?

Not One of Us

Nineteenth Sunday After Pentecost

Mark 9:38–50
Numbers 11:4–6, 10–16, 24–29

I N THE SAME WAY that it's easy to attack the religious leaders of Jesus's day, it's so easy to see the disciples and the Israelites as clueless and selfish and, generally, not understanding what Jesus or God is trying to do in the world. The disciples misunderstood almost everything Jesus said, spent their time arguing about who was greater in the kingdom, and even impeding Jesus's ministry through their actions (or inaction). The Israelites spent their time wandering through the desert complaining about the conditions, even wishing they could go back to Egypt where they supposedly had good lives (and better food), forgetting that the Egyptians enslaved them and forced them to do difficult labor.

We read this story of the disciples from the gospel of Mark, and we shake our head at the disciples, wondering how they can't see that this other person who is casting out demons in Jesus's name is doing good, even though he doesn't follow them (and it's interesting that they say he's not following "us," as opposed to Jesus, showing where their true focus might lie). They cannot understand anything or anyone outside of their limited view of the world, even going so far as trying to stop him from casting out demons from someone whom we can imagine was clearly suffering.

Of course, we take the same approach in our lives, especially within the church. We argue over nonessential issues as if they truly mattered, going beyond theological issues, such as predestination and free will, for example (as if even they really mattered). Instead, we debate worship styles, especially when it comes to what types of music we should use in worship or what kind of or whether there should be liturgical sections. We argue about budgets and buildings and carpet colors and what to hang on our walls and whether or not we should have Sunday school before or after worship (or on Sunday nights or Wednesdays or not at all). And those arguments are only within our particular church building.

We look at other churches, especially those outside of our tradition, and criticize them for what they are or aren't doing. We complain that another church has spent their money to build a new gym, as we believe that money could be better spent to feed the hungry, not taking the time to talk to our sisters and brothers, who would explain about their new, free after-school program for children in their neighborhood. We criticize the church that moves out of their old downtown location to a new suburb without talking to them to hear about a growing number of immigrants who are moving to that suburb.

We criticize actions and motivations, as if we understand what others are thinking. In his now famous graduation speech at Bennington College, David Foster Wallace tries to encourage graduating students to look past the surface of life, using the example of standing in line at a grocery store, unhappy about a woman who's taking too long and seemingly ignoring her screaming child. He writes, "If you're automatically sure that you know what reality is, and you are operating on your default setting, then you, like me, probably won't consider possibilities that aren't annoying and miserable. But if you really learn how to pay attention, then you will know there are other options." Like the disciples and like the Israelites, we see the world only through our limited viewpoints, and we evaluate people based on those viewpoints rather than actually talking to them to understand why they are doing what they are doing.

We never see the disciples talking to the person who is casting out demons in Jesus's name; we only hear that they tried to stop him. We get the impression that they didn't have a conversation with him; rather, they simply told him that what he was doing was wrong. If they would have had a discussion, they might have begun to understand how he knew about Jesus, why he was casting out demons, how he had the ability to do so, given that he wasn't in Jesus's immediate circle. They would have gotten to know him as a person, not as an issue they disagreed with.

At the end of the passage from Numbers, Joshua criticizes Eldad and Medad, who are prophesying in the camp, though they were not among those selected by Moses to do so. Like Jesus, Moses understands that God works through people we often do not choose ourselves. Those other people who attend different churches, who believe differently than we do, who might not even attend church can still do God's work. They can feed the hungry and clothe the naked and heal the sick, and they can even do so in Jesus's name, even if they don't know him in the way we do.

Jesus reminds the disciples that anyone who does such a deed in his name, anyone who gives out a cup of water in Jesus's name will not lose their reward. Jesus consistently wants to move the disciples and us away from the idea that people must believe the right doctrine in order to be followers of Jesus. Instead they and we should do what is right and just—whether that's literally giving someone a drink or finding ways to nourish someone spiritually, emotionally, or mentally—as that's what Jesus calls us to do.

Rather than spending our time arguing over theological issues that, in the end, don't much matter or hurt others, we should welcome everyone who seeks to do good in this world, whether they agree with us or not. We should celebrate every action we see that lessens others' suffering, that works for justice in an unjust world. We should come back to one another and say that we saw people trying to heal the world in Jesus's name and, while we didn't recognize them, we knew they were doing God's work in the world. And we went to help.

Questions for Reflection or Discussion:

What are the unimportant debates we see both within our church and between different denominations?

Where are places we see people doing God's work in ways the church might not recognize it?

Questions Even Jesus Didn't Answer

Twentieth Sunday After Pentecost

Matthew 22:15–22

J ESUS IS A GREAT example for anyone who wants to be a teacher, or at least a certain type of teacher. Granted, he does lecture from time to time (the Sermon on the Mount or those long chapters in John), but he mainly engages people in discussion. However, whenever someone asks a question, especially a particularly difficult question, he answers with a question. Like Socrates, rather than giving his listeners a direct answer, he asks them a question or questions that will guide them to their own ideas on the subject.

Jesus often takes this approach with sincerity, but he also uses this method when he knows those who are against him (the Pharisees' disciples and the Herodians, in this case) are trying to trap him. Rather than choosing one of the two options (and they always gave only two options, as if the world works that way), Jesus's return questions avoid that binary approach and provide a different way of thinking about the subject. He's not just a model for teachers, but also for politicians, though only for those who honestly want to work for good in the world.

In this case, the question they ask Jesus seems to have no good answer. If he responds that they should follow the law and pay their taxes to the Romans, he will alienate many of his followers, especially those who hoped the Messiah would come and overthrow Rome. If he tells them not to pay taxes, though, they can take that response to the Romans, who will then imprison him and, quite likely, kill him. While Jesus knows that's where his path will ultimately lead, he will go on his terms, not someone else's.

Their question is even more complicated than it first seems, as his question about the image on the coin illustrates. The emperor presented himself as divine, and the engravings on the coins said as much. Thus, Jews should not have even had one of those coins, as doing so seemed to violate the first commandment about having no other gods before God. In fact, some scholars point out that Jesus probably asked this question to show the hypocrisy of the Jewish leaders, knowing that at least one of them would be carrying such a coin, despite the prohibition not to do so.

Jesus's questions often lead the people who were questioning him to some sort of insight, some realization of how they should live their lives (like Socrates and other great teachers and thinkers). At the end of this passage, the author of Matthew says that the questioners went away amazed, but it sounds like they were more amazed at his skill in answering the question rather than by the content of the answer. Usually, when his hearers learn something new, the authors of the gospels talk about how people were amazed at his teaching, which is not the case here. Jesus doesn't ultimately answer their question; he simply avoids their trap.

That difference could be because there is no good answer here. There is no way Jesus can provide a direct answer that won't lead him and his followers (and anyone who follows his advice) into trouble. However, people do read his non-answer as an answer, which often causes conflict in how we think about our interactions with government today. Traditionally, people read Jesus's answer as a rationale for paying our taxes to the government, no matter what it does, and living our lives in such a way that we reflect Jesus's teachings otherwise. People usually cite a few comments from Paul's letters as support for such a reading, often referencing his comments about how governments are ordained by God.

Such an approach, though, doesn't leave room for those who wish to protest the government through a denial of tax payments. There are a group of Christians, albeit small, who argue that the government should not use their tax money for actions they disagree with, usually war, but not always. The Quakers are known for their objections to war, and they work diligently to avoid any connections to war (usually through conscientiously objecting to the draft), so they might take such an approach, but they are not the only ones.

If, however, we read Jesus's comment about giving to the emperor what is the emperor's on an absolutely literal level, then those who object to supporting certain government initiatives with their tax money would clearly be going against Jesus's teachings. However, if we think about Jesus's comment a bit more, we would see that we actually owe nothing to the emperor (or government). If we give to God the things that are God's, that would be everything, including our money. However, it is rare when we hear anyone argue that we should not pay our taxes, as that money is actually God's, partly because, as with the Israelites, the punishment would be swift and clear for us.

What Jesus might ultimately be arguing with his response (besides avoiding a trap) is that the real problem for us all is that we separate our lives between the sacred and the secular at all. If everything is God's, then everything we do is connected to God. Thus, when we pay our taxes, we should do so as a sacred act. Rather than simply voting once every two or four years for politicians to make decisions of what to do with that money, we should be actively involved in the political process throughout the year to make sure that money goes to what we believe in, of how it can do God's work. We shouldn't leave those decisions up to other people without our input, and we should object to actions not in line with Jesus's teachings.

Of course, we will disagree about what those actions are. Some Christians argue that some wars are just, and they will willingly support them, not just with taxes, but with their lives. Others will oppose every war. What should guide us through all of those decisions, though, is not what political party we voted for, but how we think Jesus's teachings translate into action. When Jesus says we should feed the hungry, we have to decide how best to do that. When Jesus says that we should love our neighbor, we have to think through what that looks like. What we cannot do is stand idly by and let other people make those decisions. Everything and everybody is God's, so we have to engage every idea and every person with God's love.

Questions for Reflection or Discussion:

What problems do you see that come from the interactions between government and your faith?

Where are places where Christians should take more action, perhaps even civil disobedience, against the government?

Can't Buy Us Love

Twenty-First Sunday After Pentecost

Mark 10:17–22
Amos 5:6–7, 10–15

T HIS STORY FROM THE gospel of Mark is a well-known passage, but it's probably well-known because we spend so much time thinking about how we explain it away. It's certainly one of the passages known for making people uncomfortable, especially in America, where we pretend class and wealth don't divide us, where the best way to get elected to political office is to promise to cut taxes and increase our personal wealth. We care about money and our relationship to it a good deal, so, whenever someone seems to criticize that relationship or talk about redistributing funds, we tend to get nervous.

Part of this man's problem, though, isn't money at all; it's simply doing what's difficult for him to do, something we can all identify with. When Jesus lays out the list of commandments (quite clearly leaving out coveting), the man can confidently say that he has kept all of them, but, when Jesus asks him to do what will truly change his life, he cannot do so. Most of us have parts of our faith that come easier to us than others. Perhaps we're particularly moved by prayer or music, but we struggle to make time for any kind of study. Or maybe we're gifted at being able to convey ideas to other people, but struggle with hospitality. Maybe we are truly able to welcome the stranger, but deep relationships consistently evade us.

Jesus asks us to do what makes us uncomfortable, not because we need to be good at everything, but because we learn about ourselves and other people when we interact with others in different ways or put ourselves in situations where we're not the experts. When we have to rely on other people or stumble through an awkward encounter, we have to be honest about who we are and who we aren't. Through it all, though, as in this passage, Jesus loves us, not because we're good at something or not, but because we simply are.

Jesus loves the man in this story, as well. He loves him because he is so sincere, as it's clear he wants to do what is good and right in the world. He loves him because he has sought Jesus out, as he wants to find truth and meaning in his life. He loves him because Jesus knows he is human, and he is flawed and fallible, as we all are. However, as my current minister often includes in the liturgy, Jesus loves him too much to let him stay the way he is. Jesus accepts us as we are, but he wants us to be better.

In this case, the man has one fixation that keeps him from becoming who he can be: money. The man has clearly been successful in life, as far as most people measure success. In fact, our only real description of the man is that he has many possessions, as if that definition is all that explains him. Though he has kept those other commandments, his wealth has always guided who he is, as we let so many definitions guide who we are. We have to be the smart person or the good cook or the shrewd dealer or the athlete or whoever it is we see ourselves as. If someone or something threatens that idea of ourselves, we become defensive.

For many of us in America, wealth or career is usually involved in our definition. No matter our gender or sexual orientation or gender identity, we believe we have to make a certain amount of money either to live the life we want or to provide for our family in whatever form it takes. We are hesitant to admit that we struggle financially because, in America, we can take care of ourselves, provide for us and our own. Any admission otherwise deflates that image of ourselves that we work so hard to create, showing us to be weak and incapable.

God has a different vision of money, though, as the passage from Amos reminds us. The prophet reminds us that anytime some people have more, that means that other people not only have less, but that the system keeps them from having more. We only have "houses of hewn stone" and "pleasant vineyards" because we "trample on the poor" and "take from them levies of grain." I'm sure that most of us would deny such accusations, arguing that we are charitable and generous in our giving, that we support a number of ministries that help those who have less than we do. Such actions are good and, at times, even quite helpful; however, they ignore the systemic problems that occur.

The wage gap in America continues to widen as people at the top of companies and organizations make almost two hundred times what those at the bottom make, as income inequality is worse than any time in America since 1928, the year before the Great Depression began. Even recently, as the stock market has hit record levels, an NPR story reminds us that the top ten percent of Americans (by income) own 81% of all stocks, while the bottom eighty percent only own eight percent. Given how many retirement plans for those of us nearer the top are connected to the stock market, it's in our best interests for companies to make higher profits, no matter how they do so.

For those lower down the income level, we have to shop at big box stores or, more frequently now, online where we can get cheaper products. Of course, those products are made overseas in working conditions that are often inhumane and the pay is not enough to live on unless someone works closer to eighty hours a week. Our friends and family (and sometimes we) have to work at the places that sell those products, often for close to minimum wage and no benefits, especially as more jobs have moved to part-time, leading us to work two or three jobs to balance our personal budgets.

Jesus asked the man to break out of that system, and he calls us to do our best to do so, as well. When we can afford it, we should shop at places that pay their employees living wages and that sell products that come from companies that treat their employees well. When we can't afford to shop at such places, we should not feel guilty, but remember that, as with the man who came to learn from him, Jesus loves us as we are. Our income is not a measure of that love, no matter what its level. The one action we can all take is to focus on buying what we need, not what we want, to try to bring some sort of economic justice to our communities and our world. Income can't get in the way of Jesus's love for us; we shouldn't let it get in the way of our love for others, no matter what we have to give up.

Questions for Reflection or Discussion:

What are some things we let define us or that get in the way of our faith?

How can we change how we think about or spend money to lessen inequalities in our society?

Always Reforming

Reformation Sunday

Matthew 11:12–19

USUALLY, REFORMATION SUNDAY CENTERS around Martin Luther and the passage from Romans (in the third chapter) where he has his realization about grace as the centerpiece of Christianity. Such an approach was not in keeping with the Catholic traditions of his day, which focused much more on people's trying to earn their way into heaven, either through living a righteous life or through buying their way in, as parts of the Catholic church had become rather corrupt. Thus, the idea that everyone can find salvation through grace rather than by going through the channels of the church would not only have been revolutionary, it would have terrified the church establishment.

In the passage from the gospel of Matthew, we see the same problem in Jesus's time. The religious leaders had a particular way of viewing faith, and they expected everyone else to share that view, if they wanted to participate in religious life. Unlike today, where there are varieties of churches on the same block with each other, these religious leaders had a monopoly on religious life. If somebody was Jewish, they would need to worship in the temple, and there was only one way into the temple: the religious leaders' way.

When various prophets appeared, then, they tended to make those religious leaders uncomfortable, as they proposed new ideas, reshaped old ones, or called out the hypocrisies they saw. In some way, they didn't fit in with religious life as the leaders wanted it to be. Jesus points out, though, that the religious leaders aren't happy with either of the portrayals he and John represent. John was more of an ascetic; in fact, some scholars believe he was an Essene, a religious group that separated themselves from society and tried to live a life of purity. He certainly didn't take part in the feasts of his day, leading to Jesus's comment that he "came neither eating or drinking." Jesus, on the other hand, did go to the feasts, often those hosted by tax collectors and other sinners, but also those hosted by some of the religious leaders themselves. They were accusing Jesus of liking those feasts a bit too much.

As Jesus recognizes, there was no way of satisfying the religious leaders, as they weren't happy with John's asceticism or Jesus's enjoyment. What they wanted was for both of them to behave as the religious leaders did, which seems to be to attend the feasts that they put on, but not those other people did. John didn't participate in theirs, so they were unhappy; Jesus participated in everyone's, so they were unhappy. They wanted their version of moderation.

The church today also likes the idea of moderation, as we, too, are frightened by those who live on the extremes of issues. Someone could also come into the church with different ideas of how to do church. They might want to sing different songs or sing more or not sing any at all or sing with more or no instruments. They could want to include children in worship in more extreme ways, maybe put them in the middle of the sanctuary (assuming we even have what we call a sanctuary) instead of in the nursery. Perhaps they want people to stand up and tell personal stories, honest accounts of where they struggle and succeed, rather than having the minister stand up and preach a twenty-minute (or more) sermon every week. They might come with ideas we haven't even thought about yet, types of worship we can't imagine because we have spent most of our lives in the church, and we have always done it the same way.

When it comes to social justice, we certainly say we believe in it, but we don't want people to use the church to push their agenda, and we definitely don't want people marching in the streets in our name, even ending up in prison. We say we want to welcome anyone into our churches, but then someone visits who isn't as like us as we're comfortable with, perhaps it's someone of a different race or socioeconomic status, or maybe it's someone who's LGBTQ, maybe even someone who doesn't identify as any gender and asks us about bathrooms and pronouns, or it could even be someone who needs different types of access to even get in the building or get around in it and who also asks us about bathrooms, but for different reasons of accessibility.

All of these new ideas and new people make many of us nervous, as we want church to be the way it has been for as long as we've been involved with it, whether that's a few months or our entire lives. We're people who want to be comfortable, like the religious leaders, people who want to live in the middle ground where the majority of people will be happy. New ideas and new people will only lead to conflict and chaos, we think, so we're better off staying how we are.

But new ideas and new people lead to the reformation of the church, whether it's the new ideas that came from John and Jesus or from Martin Luther or from Oscar Romero or from Martin Luther King, Jr., or from Nadia Bolz-Weber. Jesus doesn't want the church to stay the same because Jesus doesn't want the world to stay the same. If we are going to affect the world in any meaningful way, we have to open our ears and hearts to the new ideas and new people God brings to our churches. We cannot be the church we were in the 1950s or the 1990s or even 2010 and impact the world in a meaningful way. We have to be an ever-reforming church, changing not with the times, but ahead of them, moving the world in ways it needs to go, not simply reacting to changes years, even decades later.

Such an approach will make us all uncomfortable. It is easier to live with the ways we have always been the church, but *easier* is not what Jesus has called us to. We have to live in the midst of the discomfort, but we will live there with each other, pushing one another to try new ideas, bringing new people into the church, worshiping and serving in ways we couldn't have imagined months before. We will let God change the church because we know we need changing. We will let God change the church because we know the world needs changing.

Questions for Reflection or Discussion:

What are some times your congregation has changed and seen benefits from doing so?

Where are places you and/or your congregation need to continue to change? If we want church to be a safe space for people, who gets to decide what that means?

The Heart of God

Twenty-Second Sunday After Pentecost

Matthew 23:1–12
Exodus 3:1–15

THESE PASSAGES FROM THE gospel of Matthew and the book of Exodus show us two different ways of interacting with God. The scribes and Pharisees dictate how others should behave, giving the people guidelines and commandments that are almost unbearable, while they do not practice them themselves. Jesus, as he often does, criticizes the religious leaders not so much for their beliefs, but for their hypocrisy in how they act out (or don't) those beliefs. They are much more focused on how people perceive them than in the connection between their actions and the truth of their hearts.

The main problem with the scribes and Pharisees here, then, is that they claim to speak for God while misrepresenting themselves. Jesus doesn't criticize them for the actual teachings—he even tells his listeners to do what the religious leaders teach—but, when one speaks on behalf of God, expectations follow from that position. Since they support their arguments by calling on the name of God, referencing what the authors of the Torah wrote, the people should expect them to live up to those commandments themselves. They should live out their faith, not just express it in speech.

Moses sees much more clearly than the religious leaders do. He sees the sacred in the world around him, which is what ultimately enables him to speak on behalf of God. When he sees the burning bush, he turns toward it, moving from the path to see why the bush does not burn up. The author of Exodus even writes, "When the Lord saw that [Moses] had turned aside to see, God called to him out of the bush . . . " God doesn't call Moses until he steps out of his normal path and wants to see what is different about this bush. He looks beyond his everyday world to see something supernatural.

Then, when God does call on Moses to speak in God's name, he is hesitant to do so. Part of Moses's reaction is certainly fear, as other passages in Exodus make clear. Moses tries to get God to send someone else, even involving his brother Aaron in the discussion, rather than simply responding, as many others in the Bible do, "Here am I." However, Moses also reacts with hesitation because he knows it is an awesome and fearful task to speak on behalf of God. Rather than reacting with enthusiasm, Moses's first reaction is to ask what right he has to go to Pharaoh and speak on God's behalf.

We know that Moses has courage to work for the good of his people, as he previously killed an Egyptian who was beating an Israelite. That action may have been rash, but it shows that Moses has something within him that he just needs to have drawn out of him, as God will ultimately do. Moses is far from perfect, but he at least recognizes the sacred underpinnings of the world, which is why he sees the challenge of speaking on behalf of God much more than the religious leaders of Jesus's day do.

We live in a world where people seem all too willing to speak in the name of God, almost always using that name to justify what it is we want to accomplish. We hear politicians invoke God's name to attack other countries, to stop people who are different than we are from coming into our country, to pass legislation that disenfranchises an entire swath of people while protecting those who look like they do. We hear ministers and lay Christians use God's name to oppress others who don't look like them or love like them, to keep certain segments of the population out of leadership or positions of power, to keep people out of their churches instead of welcoming them in.

All of these actions, as with the religious leaders of Jesus's day, stem from a place of pride, a belief that we know what God thinks, who God loves, how God loves. There is a famous quote from Anne Lamott where she writes, "You can safely assume you've created God in your own image when it turns out that God hates all the same people you do." Those who are vocal about what God wants in this world are usually the people who simply use God's name to move people to accomplish what they actually want to see in the world, not who are actively working for God's kingdom.

Moses acts out of humility, fearful of what it means to speak on behalf of God, knowing he will not live up to such a calling. And he doesn't. He makes numerous mistakes throughout his life, but he constantly tries to draw the people back to God and God back to the people. The religious leaders of Jesus's time believe they know exactly what God expects of the people, and they don't hesitate to tell them. They, too, make numerous mistakes, but because of their pride, they lead people away from God.

In the same way, people who speak today, knowing what and how God thinks, turn people away from the church. When they loudly proclaim that God loves these people and hates those, that there are sins God will not forgive, that there are people God will not welcome, they push people away. One of my former ministers regularly said, "We do not know the mind of God; we do know the heart of God." Throughout the scriptures, God repeatedly upends our expectations, accepting those whom society deemed unacceptable, loving those the religious leaders called unlovable. We should remember that God continues to do so, that God will repeatedly defy and exceed our expectations. And that should keep us humble whenever we're using God's name.

Questions for Reflection or Discussion:

When are some times you have heard people speaking in God's name, both positively and negatively?

Where are some places we should, albeit humbly, speak in God's name?

A False Choice

All Saints Day

> Matthew 5:1–12
> I John 3:1–3
> Revelation 7:9–17

ALL SAINTS DAY IS one of those days many of us grew up without much, if any, knowledge of. We were usually focused on the night before, All Hallow's Eve or Halloween, which had no religious connection for many of us. Instead, the day after Halloween was simply the day we recovered from staying up too late and eating too much candy, the two often clearly connected, as the sugar kept us from sleeping as long as we normally would have. The only saints we were thinking about were those people who gave out the really good candy or who had hot chocolate waiting for us on those cold evenings.

Even in the church, many denominations ignored All Saints Day for years, at least within the Protestant tradition. If you grew up Catholic or Orthodox or Episcopalian or Lutheran, then you knew all about saints and the day of their celebration, but, for those of us who grew up in either the evangelical or some of the lower church mainline traditions, the beginning of November was no different from any other day in the long season of Ordinary Time (or the Season After Pentecost). And for some of us who grew up in the evangelical tradition, the focus was still on Halloween, as that day was when people turned their minds and hearts clearly toward evil.

We also didn't talk about saints very much, if at all. The early disciples almost all became martyrs, so we might hear a bit about their stories if the sermon happened to drift onto someone like Andrew or Thaddeus, and we might even get a mention of Stephen as the first Christian martyr when going through the book of Acts. Otherwise, though, many Protestants equated the veneration of saints with idol worship, as Jesus should be the focus of any kind of worship. Clearly, there was a lack of understanding about the Catholic and Orthodox practices, but there was (and still is) a misunderstanding of saints.

When most of us in the Protestant tradition think about saints, we have one of a few ideas. There's Mother Teresa, the one person who crossed traditions and earned the respect and almost worship of Protestants. Also, there are the martyrs, as we heard a few stories here and there, enough for us to equate saints with those long ago (emphasis on "long ago") who gave up their lives for their beliefs. We might also think about the scene in this passage from Revelation, a large multitude in heaven, dressed in white, singing and praising God. In other words, we didn't (and don't) think about anyone who is like us in any way.

We end up believing that other people are saints, that the only way to be a saint is to be incredibly sacrificial, like a Mother Teresa, or to be dead. Even in many churches today, All Saints Day includes a roll call of those who have died in the past year. While that practice is a great way to recognize those who played meaningful roles in our lives and who are no longer living, it keeps the emphasis on the dying part of being a saint. We're left with two extremes—give up everything we own and move to some place like Calcutta or die—neither of which sound appealing to most people.

However, the passages from I John and the gospel of Matthew remind us that there are two other ways we're saints. In I John, we're reminded that we are already saints, in that the word comes from the Latin verb meaning "to consecrate." The author of I John says that "we are God's children now." We are not God's children because we behave like Mother Teresa or because we aren't living any longer; we are God's children because God loves us just as we are, sanctifying us by that love. Because of that love, we desire to love and serve others, to make them holy in the same way we are holy, to remind them that they are God's children, too, simply because of God's love.

In the gospel of Matthew, Jesus clearly lays out the way in which we do that. Not all of us can be Mother Teresa, but we can all mourn with those who have lost those they love, can mourn for those who have died. We can all work for peace, to try to reconcile various people who have become estranged, to engage with everyone we meet with a peaceful spirit. We can all show mercy to people we encounter, to give them some of the grace we receive from God and from one another, no matter if we or they deserve it.

We can all hunger and thirst for righteousness, working to make the world a more just place, especially for those on the margins of our society, the ones we often overlook. If we have privilege in our society, we can stand beside and behind those who have less, using whatever power we do have to try to pass it to people who have less. Those of us who are white can stand with our minority brothers and sisters who are working for fair housing and wages and treatment by police officers and other authorities. Those of us who are straight and cisgendered can work with our LGBTQ friends who are fighting for basic rights, like what they want people to call them or where to use the bathroom, in addition to jobs and housing and marriage equality. Those of us who have different abilities than those whom society deems as less than because of how they can or can't walk or speak or move can be their allies as they fight for equal access to all areas of society.

We are already saints because of God's love, which consecrates us daily. We should then draw on that love and live out our own lives as saints by doing what we can to show others that love and grace. We can work for peace and justice, mercy and empathy, no matter who we are or where we live or how much money we make or anything else society says is important. We don't have to wait until we're dead and we don't have to move to some other part of the world. There are needs enough right where we are, while we're alive. God has made us saints; now, we should live up that term.

Questions for Reflection or Discussion:

Who would you describe as saints in your life? What made them so?

What can we do today, where we are, to live up to the title of *saint*, which we've already received?

We Shall See

Twenty-Third Sunday After Pentecost

Mark 10:46–52
Jeremiah 31:7–9

T HIS STORY FROM THE gospel of Mark seems like just one more healing story among so many. Jesus has healed the blind and made the lame walk throughout the gospels, and here we get one more. Bartimaeus is just one more person Jesus interacts with, providing a physical healing that they need, causing them to follow Jesus as he goes about his ministry. Beyond the fact that Bartimaeus has a name, nothing about this story is particularly noteworthy, just a few verses showing one brief instance in Jesus's ministry.

However, the placement of this story shows us that something else is going on in this story. In the verses before this passage, Jesus has told his disciples yet again that he is going to Jerusalem, where he will be mocked, spit upon, flogged, and killed, yet he will rise again. Instead of presenting a reaction to that information, the author of Mark shows James and John going to Jesus to ask if they can sit on his right and left hand, causing the other disciples to be angry at them for their request.

At least they seem to understand that Jesus will have some sort of kingdom beyond this world, given their request, but James and John clearly still misunderstand what Jesus has come to do. The other disciples don't do any better, as, rather than clarify for James and John what Jesus's ministry has been about, they simply respond to their base request. Essentially, they don't see Jesus clearly, despite all the time they have spent with him.

The person who does see Jesus clearly, though, is Bartimaeus, the blind beggar. He cries out for Jesus, calling him Son of David, putting him in the lineage of the Messiah. No matter how many times people tell him to be quiet, he continues to cry out, always using that phrase, Son of David. While the disciples argue and bicker over their role in Jesus's kingdom, Bartimaeus fulfills what should be their role of telling the world who Jesus actually is.

Similarly, after Jesus has healed Bartimaeus, he simply follows Jesus to wherever he is going next. He has gotten what he wanted, nothing more than sight, and now he is willing to follow Jesus. The disciples, who have gotten much more from Jesus's time on Earth, continue to squabble about who gets more. Jesus has taught them, has fed them, has walked with them, and they still can't see him clearly; it's only a blind beggar who sees Jesus for who he is and his kingdom for what it will be.

The Bible repeatedly uses sight or seeing as a metaphor for insight, as we still do today. In the gospel of Matthew, Jesus says that the eyes are the window to the soul, and we, once we understand a point, declare "I see." In Greek tradition, prophets were often blind (Tiresias is the most famous example), as they could see the truth of a world they couldn't literally see, while the rest of the people could see the physical world, but nothing beyond that.

In the same way that the disciples don't see Jesus and his kingdom clearly, we, too, miss the point. Too often, we think about what Jesus can give us rather than seeing what we already have and using that to follow Jesus. Like the disciples, we want more than what we already have rather than seeing those who have needs we could meet. While we enjoy our food and clothing and shelter, we walk past those who have little or none of those, going about our daily business rather than helping where we can, giving out of our excess.

It's easier not to see in our world, as there are needs everywhere. Almost every city has a population of homeless people who congregate in downtown areas where so many of us go, and, not only do we not help, we look past them or through them, going out of our way not to see them. Even if we are unable to help them, we choose not to see them, treating them as if they are not there, one more way people take away their humanity. When they approach us and ask for money, we turn to the side or even switch to the other side of the street to avoid having any interaction with them. Like those who were telling Bartimaeus to be quiet, we wish they would simply go away and not bother us.

Jesus, though, sees everyone, no matter their socioeconomic or housing status. He asks what people need, and he meets that need. More importantly, though, he treats people as humans, talking to them, having a conversation, healing them through love and kindness as much as through any kind of physical healing he might provide. Whether we can provide physical needs for people, we, too, can provide this kind of recognition of others' humanity.

Jesus's kingdom is not one of power and prestige, which the disciples don't understand. As the passage from Jeremiah points out, God calls the blind and the lame, those who are weeping and in need of consolation. We are those people, as we are unable to see or to walk; we mourn for the world, our families, ourselves, and we need consolation. We are broken people whom God is calling to create a kingdom where we all will then walk by brooks of water, walk in a straight path, where even the blind and lame can manage.

It's true that we don't see others as we should or see God's kingdom as it can be, but Jesus does see it clearly, and he will guide us to it, if we let him. If we, like Bartimaeus, follow Jesus, we will have glimpses of that kingdom, as even the disciples—who didn't see—did, at times. God calls us all, no matter what we currently see, either because of our blindness or because of our weeping. He will make us into a kingdom where we treat everyone with humanity and decency and equality, where we are all God's children, not because of what we do, but because of God's love for us. God's radical inclusivity binds us together, making us into a kingdom of people who see and run, spreading God's love to those who haven't seen it in their lives yet.

Questions for Reflection or Discussion:

Who are people or what are things we don't see in our cities and nations today?

What can the church do to help us and others see those people and things more clearly?

The Generous Widow

Twenty-Fourth Sunday After Pentecost

Mark 12:38–44

T HIS PASSAGE HAS ALWAYS been a popular one for Stewardship Sunday or any time a church is raising funds for much of anything. It seems perfect for such times, as the message that comes from the widow's action is clear: we should give even out of our poverty, just as the widow did. Despite their generosity, the rich people are not the ones Jesus praises, focusing instead of the poor widow. Thus, no matter how much money we have, we should give until it hurts. It's easy to see why ministers pull from this passage when they need to inspire (to put it nicely) people to give.

However, this passage seems a bit too perfect for us to believe that it's a literal event. It reads much more like a parable for a variety of reasons. First, how can we tell that the woman is a widow just by looking at her? Is she still wearing black in mourning for her dead husband? Or is there some other indicator? The same question applies to the level of income. We're supposed to know which people are rich and poor simply by looking at them. Granted, there are ways of telling income simply by looking, but it seems odd here that Jesus can tell exactly who is in which income bracket simply by watching them.

On top of that, Jesus then has time to call his disciples over to him after he sees the widow contribute (and isn't it odd that he can see exactly how much she put in?). It's unclear if the disciples see what she has done or not, as readers aren't told where the disciples even are. If he has to call them to him, then they're clearly not standing right by him, watching what he is watching. The disciples aren't known for being all that observant in the first place, so it seems that Jesus would need to explain what he was pointing out.

None of these complicating factors mean that this event didn't happen. Jesus could have seen a woman who was clearly poor and clearly a widow contribute a small amount of change, then use that story when teaching the disciples. For the sake of narrative, the author of Mark could then have changed it into the present tense to make it more immediate (which Mark's author often does). The story could also simply be a parable that Jesus told that the author changed into an actual event. In either case, the story of the widow shouldn't be read separately from what has come immediately before it. Whoever wrote down the gospels arranged their stories in particular orders for particular reasons. Part of that might simply have been to help people remember stories (a mnemonic device, essentially) when they were passed along orally, but the final author certainly could choose to change that.

Just before we get the story of the widow's offering, we get a condemnation of the religious leaders. Jesus uses them as a negative example of two main problems: pride and greed. Pride actually gets more coverage, as Jesus talks about the scribes' desire to have people see them parade around in their robes, to greet them with respect, to have the best seats at feasts, and to say long prayers. All four of these are directly connected to their faith, as their robes illustrated their place in the hierarchy of Judaism (and their sincerity), people respected them because of their piety, the feasts were celebrated on holy days, and the long prayers are rather obvious.

Thus, it is not simply pride that Jesus attacks here, but religious pride. He wants his listeners to understand that God doesn't want people to parade their faith. It is something to practice, certainly, but not for the sake of any kind of appreciation. Faith and a relationship with God are to be celebrated as things in and of themselves, and the people who practice them and God are the ones who should celebrate them. We should not seek approval in any form from other people.

The phrase about devouring widows' houses stands out, then, as being the odd one in this list. It can certainly be related to religion, as the scribes could have taken the widows' houses for the synagogue, claiming that they would use the proceeds for their work. However, since Jesus specifically mentions widows' houses, it's clear he wants us to see that the scribes are preying on the weakest members of the society, the ones who are most mentioned throughout the prophets as needing protection. In Jewish society of the time, widows had no one to protect them, so they needed the protection of the synagogue and of God.

When we move on to the next story, then, the author wants us to see a contrast here. Part of that contrast is about the greed that came up in the first section. The rich people are putting in great sums of money, while the widow puts in what little she has, a message that reinforces Jesus's condemnation of the scribes just before this story. Certainly, Jesus is talking about generosity here, but he's using an extreme example, as he often does, to illustrate his point. Jesus isn't calling for the widow or anyone else to give literally all we have to live on.

However, because of the connection with the condemnation of the scribes, Jesus is telling his listeners (and us) that they (and we) need to protect the widows of the world, those who are most vulnerable, but who, in their vulnerability, often give more than we who have much more do. The story is not simply about being generous to the church; it is about being generous to all of those around us who suffer. The rich people don't simply give large amounts of money; they don't notice the poor widow who is giving at the same time they are. They don't see the poverty around them.

As the scribes in the first section are more focused on how others perceive them, the rich people in the second simply want people to see them giving them money. They're not worried about what that money does or where it goes. It is a mindless act for them. The widow, on the other hand, is fully present in the moment, knowing why she is giving. She gives out of her love for God and humanity, not out of a desire to be seen. The rich people are so focused on others' seeing them that they do not see her.

The way to bring the kingdom is not found in how much we give, though we should certainly be generous. Instead, it is found in seeing those around us, seeing the poor and the defenseless, and finding ways to help them. As Shane Claiborne writes in *The Irresistible Revolution*, "I had come to see that the great tragedy of the church is not that rich Christians do not care about the poor but that rich Christians do not know the poor." We must move out of ourselves and our religious pride, see what others need by seeing them, then use the resources we have to help them in any way we can. That only comes through true interaction with them, not in simply dropping money in an offering plate.

Questions for Reflection or Discussion:

What are ways societal structures keep those of us who have more than enough to live on from seeing those who don't?

What are ways the church reinforces these divisions, and how can the church overcome those barriers?

True Community

Twenty-Fifth Sunday After Pentecost

Mark 13:1–13
Hebrews 10:11–25

T HE JEWS OF JESUS's day and the early Christians believed the end of
the world was coming and coming soon. Given Israel's history of oc-
cupation and wars, one can easily see why they would view the world that
way. If it wasn't a literal end of the world they expected, it was at least the
end of their world. In fact, some scholars believe the author of Mark (and
the authors of other gospels) added this passage and those like it after the
destruction of Jerusalem in 70 CE. Rather than Jesus's prophesying the end
of the world, the authors of the gospels took a literal event and connected it
to whatever Jesus did say about apocalypse.

It's not difficult for us to imagine the disciples asking this question,
given the tenor of the times they lived in. They, like us, want to know what's
coming, what the future holds for them and for us. We schedule out our
lives, planning every aspect of our lives, so we need to know what tomorrow and next year looks like. Many of our news broadcasts in all their forms
now consist of predictions of what pundits and prognosticators believe will
happen rather than their talking about what has happened.

The disciples, too, were making important decisions about their future. They wanted to know what following Jesus would ultimately lead to,
what kind of future being his follower meant. Jesus, as always, is clear on the
subject, and his response certainly couldn't have comforted them. As with
the Old Testament prophets, he predicts destruction for Jerusalem (and,
thus, for Israel), but he goes beyond that idea to talk about the persecution
his followers would face.

In the midst of these declarations, though, Jesus mentions one distraction that we tend to read over and that might help us in thinking about our future. When the disciples ask Jesus when the destruction he mentions will occur, he warns them, first, that people will try to lead them astray, that others will come in Jesus's name and try to speak for him. Clearly, Jesus is so concerned about this problem that he leads with it, waiting until later to talk about the division and persecution that will come.

It would be easy to read Jesus's concerns here as a superficial reminder that we should keep our focus on Jesus through difficult times. In the midst of personal or national or international destruction, we can simply focus on Jesus, and, as the passage from Hebrews says, he will be faithful. Nothing is wrong about such an idea, and we definitely need that encouragement from time to time. However, in this context, Jesus seems to be offering us another warning.

Jesus wants to remind the disciples and us about the importance of community, those around us who share our faith and our focus for the world. His mentioning of division just after this warning about imposters accurately predicts the history of the church more than his comment about the destruction of Jerusalem. Throughout the history of the church, we have fought with one another more than anyone else, turning against each other, especially during challenging times.

The passage from Hebrews points out, though, how Jesus connects to the expectation of community. The author of Hebrews takes the traditional view of Jesus's death as a sacrifice for the sins of humanity, but then ends with a reflection on the importance of that sacrifice by showing us how we should live together. Rather than turning against one another, we should "consider how to provoke one another to love and good deeds." "Provoke" is an interesting verb here, much stronger than a verb like "encourage." We often have to push each other, make one another uncomfortable in order to move us to love.

It would be much easier for us to let everyone go their own way, to live and let live, but Jesus wants a community that forces us to live better lives, not solely for our own good, but for the good of the world. Such an approach means that we ask questions of each other and our institutions that make someone, if not everyone, uncomfortable, to remind us of our real mission of loving the world. It means we ask each other to perform tasks and take on roles that we might not feel we can do in order to stretch ourselves and each other to become more compassionate and empathetic.

Rather than fighting with one another, we should provoke one another toward more loving relationships, especially with those who are not like us. The church is a community of people who have at least their faith in common; otherwise, we come from different backgrounds and experiences and parts of the world. We have to create a climate where all of those people are welcome, while also encouraging all of us to share our stories and thoughts, no matter how uncomfortable they make us. If we demand conformity or discourage those on the edges of the church from contributing, we end up with peaceful, meaningless community centers.

Instead, we want to be places where people can come and see reflections of Jesus, not imposters, where they can see imperfect people trusting and loving one another, especially those who do not look like them or share their political beliefs or even agree on theology. To truly show others Jesus, we need a community where we focus on who Jesus truly is rather than one where we get distracted by the divisions so prevalent in the world. We meet together to encourage one another, to provoke one another, but, always, to love one another.

Questions for Reflection or Discussion:

Where have we seen (and still see) the church fighting within congregations or denominations or the church at large?

How can we provoke each other in ways that help us overcome those divisions?

The Sheep and the Goats

Last Sunday After Pentecost

Matthew 25:31–46

WHEN I WAS A teenager, I attended a rather traditional, fundamental-ist church (Independent Christian Church/Churches of Christ—we were the ones with music, but not women in leadership). I should also quickly add that I made this move of my own free will, as I moved to fun-damentalism by my choice. My parents didn't force me in this direction. In such a tradition, as many people know, if they attended such a church, the emphasis was often on believing the right thing. In fact, there was a fear of focusing on what we did, as that would lead to a belief in salvation by works, not by grace.

Many people in such traditions try to balance this problem by point-ing to the book of James, where that author writes that faith without works is dead. That way, they argue, salvation still comes completely through God's grace, but we respond to that grace by acting as God would have us to act. This balancing act isn't limited to more conservative denominations, though. Many of us in mainline denominations also ask why we perform acts of service and love. Many of us also use the argument that we do so because God first loved us.

That approach works perfectly well, but it shifts the emphasis in a way that can make us uncomfortable. It doesn't exactly move us to these acts as a form of payback for what we have received, but it comes awfully close to doing so. If we're only loving others because God first loved us, then we're only doing it out of some sense of obligation, as if some parent did something good for us, so now we have to do something good for a sibling. It doesn't spring from a place of love.

Further complicating this parable for us contemporary readers is the idea that the people in the parable behaved the way they did out of ignorance. Both the sheep and the goats are confused by Jesus's comment that they either did or did not help him in some way, as they didn't do or not do these actions because Jesus told them to do so. Instead, they behave the way they did out of some other motivation that the author of Jesus does not clearly lay out. We don't know why the righteous helped Jesus, nor do we know the reasons the goats would give for why they didn't help those in need.

We, however, have read this parable, so we know when there is someone who is hungry or sick that we should feed them or visit them. We are unable to respond to Jesus out of ignorance. Thus, we become caught in a trap of motivation. When we see people who are hungry and feed them, we often wonder whether we are doing so because we sincerely want to help them, that we are moved in some way by their plight, or because we know that God wants us to help them, so we do.

What I've begun to believe over the past few years, though, is that that distinction doesn't really matter all that much. It's the difference between dogma and praxis. Dogma is a set of beliefs that we hold, the set of beliefs we see as true. When we say the Apostles Creed or an affirmation of faith, we are asserting dogma. If we argue about the nature of Jesus as human or divine or some sort of combination, we are arguing about dogma. When I was a teenager, we debated whether or not one had to be baptized to go to heaven, a question about dogma.

Praxis, however, is about process, not about belief. It is when we enact or embody a theory or skill. Aristotle differentiated between theoretical (dogma, essentially), poietical (production), and practical (praxis), the end goal of which was action. If we approach this parable through the lens of praxis, what becomes important is what the sheep and the goats did, not why they did it. The same can be true about our actions. Even if we behave out of strictly selfish notions (our own salvation, say), the hungry still get fed and the sick still get visited.

This approach sounds crass, but Jesus seems much more focused on praxis than he does on dogma. He upends dogma at every turn in the gospels, healing people on the Sabbath, proclaiming that the thief on the cross will be with him in paradise, interacting with the unclean. Instead, what matters for him is the result of our actions, not the motivation behind that action. When he encounters Zacchaeus, who then forgives a variety of debts, he doesn't ask Zacchaeus why he did so; he simply celebrates the action. In this parable, he doesn't ask the goats why they didn't help those in need, nor does he ask the righteous why they did. He simply says that they performed these actions, which leads to their reward or punishment.

This parable is, in fact, the only portrayal we get of the final judgment from Jesus's perspective. Despite what we often hear about such a final judgment, the emphasis is solely on what they did; there's no discussion at all about what they believe. There's nothing, for example, about their belief that Jesus is human or divine or that he's the Messiah or the Son of God. He doesn't seem to care if they've repented of their sins or prayed what some people call the sinner's prayer. Unfortunately, we spend too much of our time these days arguing over points of theology rather than spending that energy feeding the hungry and visiting the sick.

Part of the reason is that dogma is easier to debate, and we love to debate. We want to understand the why behind something, we argue, before we act upon it. We're like the man in the Buddhist *koan* whom someone shoots with a poisoned arrow. When someone offers to get help, he stops them and begins a long list of questions (such as who shot the arrow, where the feathers on the arrow originated, and what wood the shaft is made of). Of course, he would certainly die before receiving the answers to those questions. Jesus wants action from us; he wants to see the kingdom come, on earth as it is in heaven. His portrayal of that kingdom is one where everyone is welcomed, where everyone is fed (he often uses the image of the banquet or feast). Thus, his portrayal of who receives welcome and who receives punishment is based solely on whether or not people try to bring the kingdom to earth. That's much more important than what they believe.

Questions for Reflection or Discussion:

What are points of theology the church spends much of its time arguing about today?

Where are places in our communities and our world where we can spend that energy acting out the kingdom?

Books and Movies I've Read and Seen That Have Helped Me

I COULD MAKE THIS LIST much longer, especially if I include more books or movies from recent years, or if I included novels that have definitely shaped my thinking. It's clear from this list that much of my development happened in the late 1990s and early 2000s, so know that bias exists. There are, I'm sure, a range of interesting works published in the past two decades that I'm simply not familiar with. Here, though, are books and a few movies that helped shape my thinking about faith and how it should impact my life.

Bancroft, Anne, editor. *The Dhammapada*. Vega, 2002.

Bawer, Bruce. *Stealing Jesus: How Fundamentalism Betrays Christianity*. Penguin Random House, 1997.

Borg, Marcus J., editor. *Jesus at 2000*. Westview Press, 1997.

Bringas, Ernie. *Going by the Book: Past and Present Tragedies of Biblical Authority*. Hampton Roads, 1996.

Coates, Ta-Nehisi. *Between the World and Me*. Spiegel and Grau, 2015.

Coffin, William Sloane. *The Heart is a Little to the Left: Essays on Public Morality*. University Press of New England, 1999.

Crossan, John Dominic. *Who Killed Jesus? Exposing the Roots of Anti-Semitism in the Gospel Story of the Death of Jesus*. HarperCollins, 1996.

Dyson, Michael Eric. *Tears We Cannot Stop: A Sermon to White America*. St. Martin's Press, 2017.

For the Bible Tells Me So (DVD). Dir. Daniel Karslake. Atticus Group and VisionQuest Productions. 2007.

Funk, Robert, et al. *The Five Gospels: What Did Jesus Really Say?* HarperCollins, 1996.

The Gospel of Thomas. HarperCollins, 1992.

Hanh, Thich Nhat. *Living Buddha, Living Christ*. Riverhead Books, 1995.

Norris, Kathleen. *Amazing Grace: A Vocabulary of Faith*. Riverhead Books, 1998.

Pagels, Elaine. *Beyond Belief: The Secret Gospel of Thomas.* Ballantine Books, 2003.

Pine, Red, editor and translator. *The Tao Te Ching.* Mercury House, 1996.

Prothero, Stephen. *American Jesus: How the Son of God Became a National Icon.* Farrar, Straus & Giroux, 2003.

Solnit, Rebecca. *Men Explain Things to Me.* Haymarket Books, 2014.

Solnit, Rebecca. *The Mother of All Questions.* Haymarket Books, 2017.

Spong, John Shelby. *Here I Stand.* HarperCollins, 2000.

Spong, John Shelby. *Why Christianity Must Change or Die.* HarperCollins, 1998.

The 13th. Dir. Ava DuVernay. Kandoo Films, 2016.

Thompson, Marjory. *Soul Feast: An Invitation to the Christian Spiritual Life.* Westminster John Knox, 1995.